Working in Business: A BTEC First Workbook

Alistair Norman, BTEC Coordinator, Burnley College
Marie Norman, Senior Lecturer,
Bolton Institute of Higher Education

Editor **Reg Chapman**, Principal, Oldham College

Pitman

PITMAN PUBLISHING
128 Long Acre, London, WC2E 9AN

A Division of Longman Group UK Limited

© Alistair & Marie Norman and Reg Chapman 1991

First published in Great Britain 1991

British Library Cataloguing in Publication Data

Norman, Alistair
  Working in business: a BTEC first workbook.
  1. Business enterprise
  I. Title II. Norman, Marie III. Chapman, Reg
  338.6

  ISBN 0-273-03460-X

Printed and bound in Great Britain

Typeset by 🔺 Tek-Art Ltd, Addiscombe, Croydon, Surrey

CONTENTS

Introduction   iv

Part A Getting started on your course   1
Unit 1   You and your course   3
Unit 2   Competent for the job   12
Unit 3   Starting your course   28

Part B Business support systems   39
Unit 4   Health and safety   41
Unit 5   Getting organised – filing   47
Unit 6   Business communications   55
Unit 7   Data processing and information processing   76
Unit 8   Petty cash and invoices   87
Unit 9   Stock handling   100
Unit 10   Mail handling   103
Unit 11   Reprographics   111
Unit 12   Liaising with callers and colleagues   115
Unit 13   Providing information to customers/clients   122
Unit 14   Assignments and activities   127

Part C Performing your role at work   159
Unit 15   Finding a job and knowing your rights   161
Unit 16   Using resources with care   182
Unit 17   Fitting into your organisation   189
Unit 18   Making your organisation look good   197
Unit 19   Keeping your customers satisfied   202
Unit 20   Assignments and activities   206

Part D Where next?   213
Unit 21   Options after BTEC First   215

INTRODUCTION

How can this book help you?

This book is designed to cover the most important part of your BTEC First Diploma in Business and Finance known as the **core** (this is the compulsory part of the course). It is not just a textbook containing facts and theories for you to learn. It is a workbook which means that, as well as providing facts and theories for you to use, there are many practical activities and tasks for you to complete, together with tips on how to approach them. These activities and tasks may be used to assess how well you do on the course or in class as practice. By working through them you will be able to cover the content of the course and gain the knowledge that you need, though often your lecturers will provide additional information.

You can use the workbook in several ways:

1 To read up in advance a topic on your course.
2 To check what you already know about a topic.
3 To go over something that has given you problems.
4 To catch up on work that you have missed.
5 To practise skills and tasks so that you can become very good at them and achieve high grades.

What is in the book?

Part A   Getting started on your course

Unit 1 tells you about BTEC and about the First Diploma course and the idea that the course is organised around what you can do rather than what you just write about or talk about.

Unit 2 tells you what you have to do to pass the core of the course and explains some of the ways to show what you can do.

Unit 3 covers what you will want to know about your centre (the centre is the place where you are doing the course) and your course. A lot of this information you will need to find out from your tutors but this is a handy summary. It also helps you to think about yourself and other people on your course and gives you some advice on the skills and tasks needed to get you started.

Part B   Business support systems

This part of the book helps you to do the jobs that you would find in an office and provides you with assignments and tasks to practise the clerical tasks from filing to reprographics, from dealing with customers to opening the mail. In each unit there are activities for you to learn the various clerical tasks. At the end of this part of the book are some larger assignments involving several clerical tasks – which is mostly how it is in a busy office.

Part C   Performing your role at work

This part of the book helps you to see how you fit into a business and the rights and responsibilities that you have at work.

Part D   Where next?

The final part of the book asks: 'What do you do after the First Diploma? Another course? A new job? Your own business?' This unit looks at what you can do and helps you to decide what is right for you.

This set of units aims to:

- *Encourage you to think about different types of office jobs.*
- *Tell you about your BTEC First Diploma in Business and Finance – what it contains, how you learn on the course and how you will be assessed.*
- *Give you the basic information you need to settle into your course quickly.*
- *Help you to study and plan your work so that you will do well on the course.*

Getting started on your course

To do well on your BTEC First Diploma in Business and Finance you need to know how the course is organised, what it contains, and what is expected of you. Units 1 and 2 aim to give you detailed information about this. You also need to be able to study effectively and plan your work so that you can make the most of your time; this is contained in Unit 3. Unit 3 also deals with some information about the facilities and staff you may find at the centre where you study and suggests information for you to find out yourself. You are encouraged to think about yourself, your strengths and weaknesses, and to draw up an Action Plan to help you with your studies and your future. You are also asked to find out

about the other students in your class so that you feel comfortable with them and can give help and support to each other throughout the course.

YOU AND YOUR COURSE

This unit is designed to:

- *Tell you about the different levels of BTEC course.*
- *Explain how your course is organised.*
- *Help you to choose the best options for you.*

A foundation for business

This course is a foundation for all BTEC courses in business studies. The illustration shows the different levels of courses – First, National and Higher National.

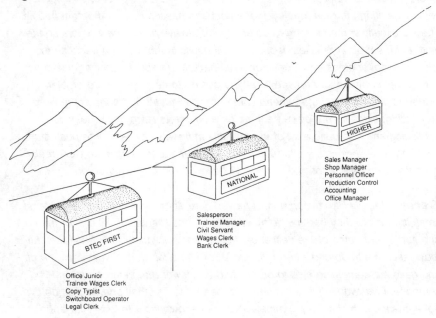

Sales Manager
Shop Manager
Personnel Officer
Production Control
Accounting
Office Manager

Salesperson
Trainee Manager
Civil Servant
Wages Clerk
Bank Clerk

Office Junior
Trainee Wages Clerk
Copy Typist
Switchboard Operator
Legal Clerk

Fig 1.1 Levels of BTEC courses

Jobs

You may already be in a job like one of those listed in Fig 1.1 and want to get a promotion, or you may be hoping that this course will get you into a worthwhile job to start your career in business. Whichever is the case you will probably be working in an office of some sort for at least part of your time. The type of work that you do will vary according to the sort of place that you work in but there are some things about office work that are the same in almost every office.

Read the two accounts of Tariq and Tracey below.

Tariq: I started here last year from college. I wasn't really sure what I wanted to do and an office job seemed to be a good idea. It meant that I would be using what I had learned at college and at school. Also it sounded interesting as they said that they wanted someone to do a lot of different jobs rather than sticking to one thing. When I first started I found it a bit strange because it's only a small firm and they left me to get on with jobs – you know, they just said 'Tariq, can you send a price list to Nelson's, and put in a covering letter to remind them that prices will go up at the beginning of the month after next. You can get the address from the files in the sales section.' That meant that I had to learn where to find things and to use my common sense a bit as well. I've pretty well got to know everyone now so I can find things out a lot faster than when I started and was scared to ask. It's a good job because I get the chance to see what goes on in all sorts of different areas and because most days are different. On a typical day I'll spend some time filing after I've dealt with the post and passed it on to the right people. There's usually some copying to do and we're always getting new orders so they have to be set up in the files. It can be a bit hectic in the morning because the telephone never stops some days and you have to be able to answer questions, calm people down a bit and see what you can do to help if there's a problem. I started to use the computer when I came here because I had done some word processing; since then they've sent me on a course to learn about desktop publishing and I do quite a lot of the publicity materials now – not the posh stuff but things like price lists so that they look smart. It's a good place to work really, even if you do have a lot to do; if I didn't have a lot to do I'd get bored.

Tracey: I really like my job here, I moved here about three months ago from a small firm where they had me doing all sorts of jobs like writing letters for the boss and sorting out some of the deliveries. I didn't know anything about half the stuff they asked me to do and when I did get stuck into a job they always took me off it and gave me something else to do or I had to answer the phone or go and find someone. I like working in a big firm a lot better than a small one. In this job I've got a chance to make the job mine – I've got my own work to look after and I organise my day so as to do it. At first it took me ages and I made some mistakes as I've never worked much with computers. I'm getting good at it now. In fact the other day the section head said that I was getting on far better than she would have expected for the time that I've spent in the section.

My job here is to deal with queries on orders and that means that I have to go through the post when it arrives and take any letters querying orders up to the section, then I call up the files on the computer and see what is wrong – usually it's just that an amount has been misread and I have to write and apologise and arrange for the right goods to be sent. Sometimes though, I have to phone the people up to find out exactly what the problem is if they haven't given all the details in the letter. You do get the odd one who gets stroppy but you have to stay polite and usually they calm down if you're nice to them. I'm going on a training *course next week to do with the new accounts system which we're getting next year and it will mean that I have to use a different computer and I'm going to be helping to train some other people on it. I'm a bit worried about it but I've got plenty of time before I have to use it for real. I like having my own job here and knowing what I've got to do and the people in the section are really nice, I haven't really met any people from elsewhere in the company but I suppose I will eventually.*

You will have seen that a lot of what Tariq and Tracy have to do are the same, and they both enjoy their jobs. Tariq likes working in a small firm and yet Tracey did not – try to write down what you think Tariq likes about working for a small firm and what Tracey disliked. Now write down what Tracey liked about the bigger firm.

What sort of firm or job would you like? Try to think about what you want from a job and make a note of what you decide. A few ideas are listed to get you started.

I like to know what I'm doing.	I like a bit of variety in work.
I want to get really good at one job.	I want to try a lot of things.
I like to have a routine.	I get bored if I have the same thing to do all the time.
I would like to work with a lot of people.	I would like to work with a few people and get to know them well.
I want to work with computers.	I do not want to have to use computers.

The activity above should have given you an idea of the job that you want to do and the type of firm that you want to work in – you may change your mind as you go on work placement and see what jobs are actually like. Whatever job or business you are attracted to, you need a sound foundation of knowledge and skills from your course.

What does your course contain?

Like all BTEC courses, the First Diploma contains 'core', or compulsory subjects, and others where you have a choice of what you study, which are called options. On BTEC courses the subjects are called 'modules', and you have to take three core modules:

Business support systems 1 – comprising ten basic clerical tasks found in most offices, such as dealing with customers and clients, or keeping financial records.

Common skills – consisting of seven skill areas which people use in any job, such as working with others, numeracy or communication.

Work role – dealing with how you fit into the organisation and how the organisation fits into the local community and the business world at large.

Together these core modules, which make up around two thirds of your course, are titled 'Working in Organisations' as they provide a foundation for anyone seeking an office career in any organisation in the public or private sectors.

In addition to the core you will take one of three main option routes. Each route prepares you for a different type of career in business: in finance, in secretarial work, or in general administration. Each route comprises two elements:

1 *Business support systems 2*, which includes the higher level clerical tasks common to the three option routes. For example, it includes important elements of information processing using a computer which are more advanced than anything in Business Support Systems 1 and are needed in all three option routes.

2 *Specialist option modules* in Finance, Administration or Secretarial. You can only take one option route at a time.

Together, the core and your chosen option route will give you your First Diploma in Business and Finance. In addition to the core and option modules it may be possible to take some additional subjects, though they do not count as part of your BTEC Diploma. Certainly full-time students will have enough time to take extra subjects. Apart from Finance, Administration and Secretarial options there are other BTEC options that are not so closely linked to a particular career, but will still be very useful to you, such as:

■ sales
■ production
■ languages.

The components of the BTEC First Diploma which you take are summarised in Table 1.1.

Table 1.1.
Components of
BTEC First Diploma

CORE – Working in Organisations	OPTION ROUTES	WORK EXPERIENCE
Business support systems 1 (Clerical Tasks) (2.0) and Common skills (1.0) and Work role (1.0)	Business support systems 2 (Clerical Tasks) (1.0) and Finance (1.0) or Administration (1.0) or Secretarial (2.0)	Block or Day release to work or Employment and day release to college

Additional studies (not part of Diploma) – other BTEC options such as Sales, Production or Languages; GCSEs; or other studies which support the BTEC Diploma

You can see that under each module there is a number, either 1.0 or 2.0. This is called the 'module value', which tells you roughly the amount of time you have to spend on it. A module valued at 2.0, like the Secretarial option will probably take you twice as much study time as one with a value of 1.0, like Finance or Common skills. But don't treat these numbers too literally as they are only a rough guide.

By simple arithmetic, in order to gain a BTEC First Diploma in Business and Finance you need to get six module values, or even seven if you choose the Secretarial option route. The reason for needing the extra module for the Secretarial option is not that it is of a higher or harder standard, or even that there is more of it. It is simply that to become good at secretarial work, especially keyboarding, it takes a lot of time and practice.

Options for jobs

The main purpose of the options is to make you competent in particular types of job. You will have seen from the table above that there are three main options you can take:

- financial work
- administration
- secretarial work.

Each of these is designed to help you towards a particular career and give you the skills and knowledge that you will need to do a job in that area. Table 1.2 shows the typical tasks you will tackle in each of the options and the kind of work that the option could lead to:

Table 1.2.
Option
opportunities

OPTION ROUTE	TYPICAL TASKS	TYPICAL JOBS
Finance	Handling payments	Cashier
	Using business forms	Accounts clerk
	Working on wages	Wages clerk
	Keeping financial records	Assistant in finance section
Administration	Reception and dealing with visitors	Receptionist
	Handling phone calls	Telesales
	Handling computer data by phone	Data processing section junior
	Setting up meetings	Junior secretary
	Arranging travel	Trainee for post as personal assistant
	Handling payments	Cashier
Secretarial	Handling phone calls	Telesales
	Handling computer data by phone	Data processing section junior
	Reception and dealing with visitors	Receptionist
	Word processing	WP operator
	Shorthand or audio	Junior secretary Copy typist
	Setting up meetings	Junior secretary
	Arranging travel	Trainee personal assistant

It does not cover all the jobs that you could do but it does indicate the jobs that a particular option route will lead to.

Choosing your options

Read the descriptions below of the different option routes and options and choose your best combination of options for the sort of job you want. It may be helpful to look back at the first activity where you thought about the sort of job that you want and to discuss your thoughts with your tutor.

1 *Finance* – covers the tasks involved in working in a finance or payroll section.

2 *Secretarial* – covers secretarial duties such as word processing, shorthand or audio and helping with meetings.

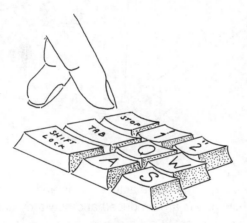

3 *Administration* – quite a lot of jobs in an office are concerned with helping to arrange things such as meetings and travel or handling information like phone calls, computer data and visitors.

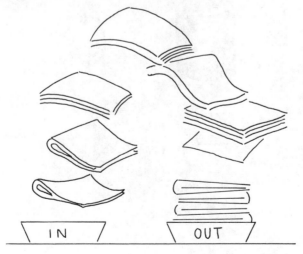

In addition to the three option routes, you might want to consider some of the following BTEC options.

4 *Sales* – selling and knowing how to keep track of sales is an important part of many jobs. This unit will give you a chance to learn to sell and to use the documents needed to keep track of a sale from when it is made to when you get paid.

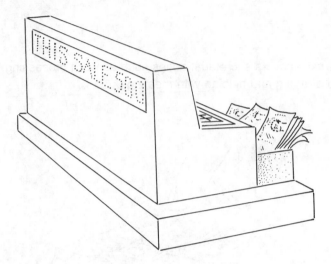

5 *Production* – many firms manufacture goods and this unit is about understanding how goods are produced and how they are distributed. After studying this you should have a clear idea of where raw materials come from and how the things you sell are made.

6 *Languages* – as we become integrated into Europe many firms are looking for people who can use another language. You do not have to be fluent but it is a real advantage to be able to speak to a foreign customer in their own language even if all you can say is: 'Thank you for calling. Can you wait a minute while I get Miss Freeman – her French is much better than mine and she'll be able to help you.'

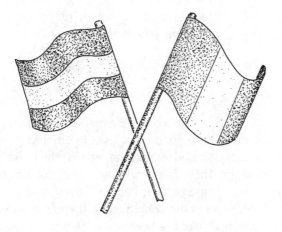

Summary

1 *There are three levels of BTEC courses – BTEC First, BTEC National and BTEC Higher National.*

2 *The BTEC First Diploma in Business and Finance is a foundation course.*

3 *The course contains two parts; core and options.*

4 *The Core has three elements Business Support Systems 1, Common Skills and Work Role.*

5 *There is a variety of option routes such as Secretarial, Finance, Administration and other options such as Sales, Production and Languages.*

COMPETENT FOR THE JOB

This unit is designed to tell you:

- *What a 'competence' is.*
- *How to prove you are competent at a task.*
- *What you will study on your course.*
- *How you will learn.*

Your course is aimed at giving you the skills and knowledge you need to be a good employee. In order to get the most out of the course, you need to understand the way in which the course works and how you will learn. This unit aims to tell you about the 'competences' that you have to learn, and how to go about proving that you can do a job. It also covers the content of the course (so you know what you will be learning in the core) and explains how you will learn and be assessed on the course.

What is a competence?

Courses that you have taken in the past have probably concentrated mainly on what you know – if you knew something and could write essays about it you could get a good pass. Your BTEC First course is also concerned with learning what you need to know to get on well in a job and career but you will also be expected to use what you know and put it into practice. So, if you have learnt about keyboarding (using different types of keyboard) then you will have to actually use a keyboard to prove that you are competent. After all, if you cannot do the job you will not be much use at work.

There are many competences that you need to get your BTEC First. They were written by employers who decided that they wanted people who were going to work in an office to be able to *do* rather than just for what they knew. Because these competences have been agreed on by employers all across the country you will get a stamp on the BTEC First that tells an employer that you are competent in a number of tasks – it is a guarantee that you can do the job. You will not get a separate diploma but your BTEC Diploma will be stamped with the NCVQ's stamp of approval.

What is NCVQ?

It is the National Council for Vocational Qualifications. NCVQ is an organisation set up by the government to make sure that training for jobs is up to a good, nationally recognised, standard – you only get their stamp of approval on courses that give you all the competences employers have agreed are needed for a particular type of job such as office work or motor vehicle work. A qualification with this stamp is called an **NVQ** (a National Vocational Qualification). Getting an NVQ is a bit like passing your driving test – it shows you are competent in both the theory and practice of driving and fit to be let loose on the road. It is also recognised nationally that you have achieved a set standard. There is a number of levels of NVQ which are based on a hierarchy of jobs. The higher up the pyramid you go, the more complicated the job becomes and the more knowledge and skill is required. Also, at the first levels it is quite easy to identify jobs that people have to do and the jobs are usually quite clear with a good deal of supervision. At the higher levels more initiative is required and there will be less supervision. When you are an office junior people check up on you more than when you are the office manager; and when you are the manager you have to supervise other people and help them as part of your job.

Your BTEC course will give you an NVQ at level 2 with a fall back of getting a level 1 NVQ.

IF YOU DO . . .	YOU GET: Business Administration NVQ
Business support systems 1	Level 1 (NVQ)
Financial route	Level 2 (Financial) NVQ
Administrative route	Level 2 (Administrative) NVQ
Secretarial studies route	Level 2 (Secretarial) NVQ

Each of these NVQs tells an employer that you are competent to do the main jobs in a particular area as described in Unit 1.

What is in your course?

To get your BTEC First award you need to show that you can do the main work tasks which are found in most offices, plus the tasks that go with the options that you have chosen. This means that you are competent to do these tasks without help. Some of the tasks are routine and you can show that you are competent to do them in a short period of time – for example, answering the phone or filing. However, some of the tasks require practice and time in order to become fully competent – tasks such as getting on with people or using a database. To prove that you are competent you have to do tasks more than once and in different situations. You may need to demonstrate you can do tasks at, for example, college and also at work.

What are the competences you have to prove?

There are three sets of competences which you need to prove to get your BTEC First core as indicated in Unit 1.

- Business support systems 1
- work role
- common skills.

You need to know what each of these parts of the core contains and the sections that follow will give you a chance to see what you have to do. It is also important to start thinking about which areas you will need to work especially hard on to become competent.

Business support systems 1

The clerical tasks are the basic clerical jobs that any office worker meets. There are 10 core clerical tasks that you will do on the core of your First award and the job of a typical office worker like Sumi in the activity that follows will involve all of these competences.

COMPETENCE	TASKS
Health and safety	Work safely and help keep the office safe.
Filing	File documents properly.
Business communications	Communicate verbally, in writing and by using the telephone.
Data processing	Use a computer, word processor or typewriter keyboard and put information into a computer.
Petty cash and invoices	Keep simple records of money coming in and going out.
Stock handling	Look after office stocks and materials.
Mail handling	Handle mail and messages coming into, and going out of, the office.

COMPETENCE	TASKS
Mail handling	Handle mail and messages coming into, and going out of, the office.
Reprographics	Use of photocopier or other way of copying documents.
Business relationships	Get on well with the people you work with and with your customers.
Providing information to customers/clients	Give customers the information they need.

Sumi works in the office of a large solicitors' practice. She is one of five staff but she is the most junior, having been with the solicitors only six months after leaving college with her BTEC First.

Look at the list of jobs that she might do in a typical day and work out which of the competences she will need to demonstrate each job. Fill in the title of the competency in the space provided – the first one has been done to give you a start.

JOB	COMPETENCES
Make several photocopies of a contract	Reprographics
Sending out bills to clients	
Covering work for John who is off sick	
Filing case notes	
Book a table for Ms Hawkins for lunch with a client	
Answer the phone	
Word process and send letters to clients	

JOB	*COMPETENCES*
Update a database of clients	
Act as receptionist at lunchtime	
Make coffee for clients waiting to see a solicitor	
Buy two rolls of sellotape using petty cash	

Work role

When you are at work you are part of an organisation – it could be a big firm, a small business, a charity or a government department. Whatever it is, there are some things you need to be able to do so that you fit into the job. People at work take on a special role – they represent the organisation and are required to help make the organisation efficient and effective and project a good image. You need to show that you are capable in all the competences listed below. They are not quite the same as the clerical tasks that you looked at in Sumi's day – you can use most of these in many different jobs.

COMPETENCE	*TASKS*
Act in accordance with rights and responsibilities of the job	**Know what rules you have to keep to when working and observe them. This will mean working safely, keeping to the rules of the firm and asking for help if you need to know what to do. You also need to know what your rights are and how to make use of them.**
Use resources with economy and efficiency	**Make sure that you do not waste time or other resources at work. You will need to keep the place tidy, be careful only to use what you need and generally take care.**

COMPETENCE	TASKS
Contribute to achieving organisational goals and objectives	You have to make sure that you do your job well if the firm is to do well. You need to make sure that your jobs are done on time, that you know how to plan to get work done and that you ask for help if you need it rather than 'muddle through.'
Contribute to change and development of the organisation	There are always changes in businesses and you need to be able to cope – by discovering information and passing it on, by looking for easier and better ways to do jobs and taking advantage of any training you are offered.
Present a positive image of the organisation	If you are good at your job, it helps the firm look good. You have to find out the right way to behave and work that way – by being pleasant to customers, by making sure you look right when meeting people and by making sure letters look good when they go out.
Provide information and advice to customers and clients	Giving customers help is important. Without them the organisation cannot work. You have to be polite, find out what you can do to help, get the right information as quickly as you can, or get someone to answer a question and pass on accurate messages if that is what they want.

Remember Sumi who works in the office of a large solicitors' practice? You have already looked at some of the jobs that she might do in a day. Now look at the list below, which will also be a part of her day, and fill in against each of the items which of the work role competences you think she is using. Fill in the title of the competency in the space provided – the first one has been done to give you a start.

JOB	COMPETENCES
Keeping work tidy	Use resources with economy
	Present a positive image of the organisation
Getting on with colleagues	
Being pleasant to clients	
Answering the phone	
Keeping to safety rules	
Writing letters	
Saving energy	
Asking for help	
Coping with new jobs/tasks	
Making phone calls	
Following rules	
Helping clients	
Helping colleagues	

You will already be able to do some of the work role competences, others you will need help with and some you may have to start from scratch. Fill in the table opposite using the scale supplied to grade how good you are at each of the competences.

A   really very good at this
B   good at it
C   OK – I can do it
D   have some problems
E   not good
F   hopeless

When you have rated yourself A–F make a note of any experience that you have in the final column as in the example given to get you started.

COMPETENCE	YOUR RATING	YOUR EXPERIENCE
Use resources with economy and efficiency	D	I am not very good at keeping to limits and I do tend to waste paper.
Act in accordance with the rights and responsibilities of the job		
Contribute to achieving organisation goals and objectives		
Contribute to change and development of the organisation		
Present a positive image of the organisation		
Provide information and advice to customers and clients		

Common skills

Common skills are those needed for all jobs. BTEC have identified seven common skills which are a vital part of all their courses. These are as follows:

1 *Working with others* – you have to be able to get on with people and work with them, even if you do not always agree with them. There are times to compromise and times to dig your heels in – you need to know which is which.

2 *Communicating* – it is no use knowing the answer to everything if you are unable to get it across to people. A badly typed, misspelled letter gives a bad impression of a business. A misleading, or forgotten phone message could cost the business money. So you need to learn to get it right – first time.

3 *Using technology* – computers, fax, mobile phones and laser scanners are all used in business to make businesses work better. You do not need to be a computer whizz-kid, but you do need to know enough to use the machines that will make your life easier and let you do your job better.

4 *Numeracy* – numbers are an important part of business (the ones on the bottom line of a payslip for example) and you have to be able to use them. Preparing quotes, invoices, working out how much your pay is – these are all times when you need to be able to make numbers do what you want to give you the information you need.

5 *Developing yourself* – as you change jobs, or see your job change, get promoted, or start your own business you will find that you need to be informed. There will be skills you need to gain, machines to operate, forms to understand. If you know how to go about keeping yourself up to date you will cope better and both you and the job will benefit.

6 *Solving problems* – there is no simple answer to solving problems but there are a few ways to make it easier to deal with them: knowing where to go for help, organising yourself so that you can see what you have to do and finding answers that have already worked for someone else or somewhere else. If you can solve problems rather than create them then you are a valuable person and you will get a lot of credit for it.

7 *Design and creativity* – some things work well, some do not. Why? Probably because what works well has been well designed; someone has put some thought into it, worked out the problems, used a little imagination and come up with a good result. It might be a form that is easy to fill in or a room layout that is safer than before – whatever it is, it works and, with some practice, you can get into the habit of good design.

If you read the following descriptions of the typical working week of Jonathan, Tanya and Winston, you will see how most of the skills above are used all the time even when the jobs they do are very different.

Jonathan *I work for a marketing firm in the main office, I have to use the computer to keep track of some of the accounts and I also have to do some desktop publishing – that can be a bit tricky as I have to take a rough sketch and make it look good. There are four of us who work in this section and we all get on well, even though there are times when we're swamped with work and we have to get really organised to get it done – tempers get a bit frayed sometimes when it's like that. I sometimes go out*

with one of the managers to a client if he has some work to do there –
usually it's producing results from some research that they've had done –
numbers everywhere! I go to college one day a week to do a BTEC
course; I want to go on to do a Higher National and get a qualification in
marketing in a few years.

Tanya I work for my parents; we run a supermarket in the town centre.
I've worked here for three years now and my parents let me do quite a lot
– I want to learn as much as I can so that I can take over some day. I
help prepare the accounts each week on the computer and I also sort out

the rotas for the checkouts and stockroom; that can take ages as people are always asking for different days or need time off and you have to work it out really carefully. I do some of the ordering now – most of the reps see my Dad to start with but I deal with some of them and I have to check what we need. There's no big problem if I buy a bit too much of something like canned food, but if you buy too much of something like eggs then you may have to throw it out and that loses money. We advertise a lot and I've started to help doing adverts, it's nice to see something you've done in the paper and looking really professional!

Winston   I set up on my own about ten months ago. I rented a stall at car boot sales for a bit before that but I've had my own stall on the market for ten months now. I have to do everything here because I can't afford any help yet. The market is only on three days so I go to the wholesalers on the others, or get the books up to date; I still do a few car boot sales on Sundays if I've had a bad week. I enjoy meeting customers and get on well with the other stallholders; when it's quiet you have a good laugh with some of them. I hate doing the books; it took me ages the first time and it was all wrong, I'm better at it now after I did a course in the evening at the college and I make sure that I keep up to date – if you don't you get in a real mess. I want to move to the five-day market next year if possible. I'll keep this stall and get someone to work on it for me if I can – that'll give me an excuse to get a flash mobile phone so I can check up on them!

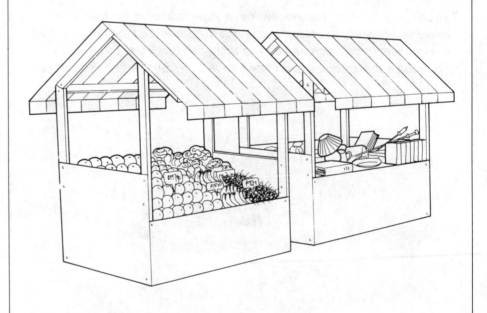

Make a list for each person of the skills that they have said they use, and when. One has been started for you.

SKILL	WHEN USED

Jonathan:
Numeracy

`Working at a client's office`
`on market research`

Tanya:

Winston:

Are there any skills
- that none of them use?
- that only one of them uses?
- that only two of them use?

You will see that common skills are those skills that are common to all jobs, though some jobs involve more or less of a particular skill. You can test this yourself by doing the activity below.

Ask five people who you know to tell you a bit about their job and see which of the skills they use. Fill the answers in below.

PERSON	JOB
1	
2	
3	
4	
5	

Skill	1	2	3	4	5
Working with other people					
Communicating					
Using technology					
Design and creativity					
Solving problems					
Developing yourself					
Numeracy					

How will you learn on the course?

> I hear, and I forget
> I see, and I remember
> I do, and I understand

The comment above sums up how you will learn on your course – by actually doing jobs as if you are at work wherever that is possible.

At school, or on other courses, you may have learnt mainly from what a teacher has said, from reading textbooks and doing projects. On this course you will certainly learn a lot from your tutors and you will also have to do quite a lot of work for yourself, but you also spend a lot of time 'doing' in order to learn. This means that you will have to work on real business problems, using real business equipment and doing tasks to the standard that you will have to reach at work. You may work on your own or with other people and you will have tutors to help and guide you, but it will be up to you to do the job. A lot of your lessons will involve you carrying out real jobs, working on a business simulation or solving business problems. The tutors will set up the jobs that you are to work on and help you to do them. Once you have done a task they will grade it to check that you have understood the main points and help you to decide what you need to practise more to improve.

Real business jobs

You will spend a lot of time doing real business jobs on the course. It will introduce you to up to date business practice and you will be expected to do many practical tasks. If you are already at work this may be a chance to get better at a job, to try tasks that are not part of your job or to find out about a different course of action – maybe a different computer package or a filing system that you have not seen before, a phone system with different facilities from the one that you normally use or a different layout for letters.

You will have to do many tasks, including:

- using office equipment
- using computers
- writing business correspondence
- preparing accounts
- keeping financial records
- preparing job adverts/job descriptions.

Actually 'doing' is a good way to learn, and by doing on the course first you get the chance to become good at a job before you try it out at work. Also, on the course you can get all the help you need to cope with anything that might give you problems at work – so make the most of the tutors, the equipment, the centre's facilities and the people in the group – you can learn a lot from them.

Business simulations

You will be spending some time working on business simulations on the course. Business simulations are exercises which are specially designed to be like real work. If you are a full time student this may take quite a lot of time. If you are doing the course part time, however, you will spend less time on simulations as you will have the chance to do some of the jobs at work. The next best thing to working in a real business is to work in a practice or simulated business in the centre. Sometimes it is even better than trying a job for the first time at work as it gives you the chance to have a go at a job or skill without the pressure of work and in a situation where you can ask your tutors for help (also it will not matter as much if you don't get it right first time). On your course you will get the chance to learn about and try different jobs by working in a simulated business or office. Full time students especially may set up and run mini-businesses as a part of their course; secretarial students may work in the centre training office. You learn in the centre what it is like in the real business world and get the chance to do jobs that you would not be given when you have just started work.

Proving you are competent

On your course you have to prove that you can do a task – show that you are competent by doing a job. You can prove that you can do a job in a number of ways:

- by doing an assignment which includes it
- by showing that you do the job at work
- by proving that you can already do it.

Whichever way you show your competence you will be expected to work to the standard that you would have to meet in a job. You will, therefore, have to be accurate in what you do, work under pressure and deal with the sort of deadlines that you get at work.

Proving you are competent through assignments

Many of the jobs that you have to do will be presented to you in the form of assignments – assignments are pieces of work which you do throughout the course and on which you are graded. These assignments are practical business tasks, partly to test what you know but also to teach you more about the jobs. You learn by doing assignments and they are a good way to have a go at a job with the chance to get some help on how you can improve.

There are many types of assignment. You may have to work in a college office, do work in groups, make a video recording or role play a scene for different assignments during the course. The assignments will include the sort of tasks you might have to perform in a real business.

Proving you can already do a job

You may be able to claim some of the competences on the course as soon as you start it if you have already had a part-time job in the past or you have previously done a course that covers some of the competences. If this is the case you need to ask the tutor in charge of the course about **accreditation of prior learning** – this means the tutor gives you credit for already having a competency. You will then not have to waste time proving you can do something again. The following is an example:

'I do a lot of typing at work and I keep the office petty cash account on a computer so I'm quite good at that. When I started at college I explained this to the course tutor and I had to do a short piece of typing that was checked. Apart from doing this I took a letter into work for my supervisor, who had to write some details of my job and agree that I worked to the right standard and sent this into the college. I also took in the printouts of the petty cash account for the last few months after having checked that this was OK. Once they had this the college signed my profile to show that I was competent in those areas.'

Summary

1 Being 'competent' is about being able to do jobs.

2 You can demonstrate that you are competent both at college and at work.

3 In the BTEC First Core you need to demonstrate competence in three areas – Business Support Systems 1, Common Skills and Work Role.

4 Clerical Tasks are the tasks a person working in an office would be required to perform.

5 Work Role competencies demonstrate that you are able to fit into the organisation, work efficiently and project a good image of the organisation.

6 *Common Skills are skills needed in many jobs.*

7 *You will learn knowledge and develop skills in practical ways, for example, working on real business problems, using business equipment and doing business simulations.*

8 *You prove you are competent to do a task by demonstrating that you can actually do it.*

9 *You can prove that you are able to do a task in several ways, for example, by doing an assignment, by doing the task as part of your work or by practical demonstration.*

STARTING YOUR COURSE

This unit is designed to:

- *Introduce you to the centre where you are studying.*
- *Introduce you to your fellow students and their strengths.*
- *Get you to assess yourself and draw up an action plan.*
- *Help you to study and plan your own work on the course.*

When you join a new course, possibly at a new centre, you have lots of questions such as:

- Where is the library?
- Who is in charge of my course?
- Where can I get a coffee or something to eat?
- What are the rules for attending classes?
- Are there any rules about health and safety?
- What are the other students in my class like?
- What facilities are there I can use?
- Who do I go to for help with work?

This unit answers the basic questions you are likely to ask in the first few weeks on the course. Equally important, you have to ask questions about yourself – what you are good at and not so good at – so that you can plan how to be successful in all aspects of the course. Finally, the unit gives you tips on how to study successfully on the course.

When you start your BTEC First course you will have an **Induction** – some time set aside to introduce you to your centre and course and get to know the staff and other students. This is vital because it gives you information to help you to settle quickly into the course and get the most from it straight away.

Your centre's facilities and health and safety

The centre is the place where you are taking the course – it may be a college, training centre, a workplace or even a school. If you are new to the centre you may be taken on a tour to show you where the facilities are

– rooms, cafeteria, computer rooms, library, toilets and offices. In all centres there are some rules and regulations, notably ones concerned with health and safety. The Health and Safety at Work Act states that you have a responsibility not to do anything which will harm other people or yourself.

You will be using different equipment and machines on your course and there will be health and safety rules to follow when using them. You need to be aware of the fire drill and are likely to be taken on one right at the beginning of the course.

Find out the following basic information about your centre:

1 List any rules and regulations which affect you as a student at the centre. Some typical house rules are given to show you the idea:
- Attendance at all classes is compulsory.
- When the fire alarm goes everyone must leave
  the building and assemble at . . . .
- This is a no smoking college. You can only
  smoke in the special areas set aside for it.

2 Where are the nearest first aiders to the rooms that you will usually use?

3 Get the information on fire procedures and ask to be taken on a fire drill if you have not already been shown what to do.

4 Where are the following facilities, and when are they open:
- cafeteria?
- college office?
- library?
- open learning rooms?

5 Is there a sports hall? If there is:
- when is it open?
- what does it offer?
- where is it?

6 Where are the student counselling and the careers service offices? When are they open?

Centre staff

Getting to know the centre staff is vital. Large centres are usually divided into departments, sectors or sections – this is because it is easier to manage. Each department (sector or section) deals with a number of courses and has someone in charge of it. This person, normally called a head of department, sector head or section head, is responsible for the smooth running of that part of the centre. There is normally someone in charge of each course. This person normally has a title such as course director, course coordinator, or course tutor. There may be a large number of students taking a course and they are split into classes. Each class has someone to look after the students. This person is sometimes called a personal tutor, tutor, group tutor or class tutor and has the responsibility of dealing with any problems you may have on the course, keeps track of your progress and attendance, and may deal with your references.

ACTIVITY

Find out the following information about the key staff at your centre. Once you have this information you will need to draw it up as a chart.

1 The name of the principal/head teacher or person in charge of the centre?
2 The name of the head of department, head of sector or head of section in which your BTEC First course is based?
3 The name of the person in charge of your BTEC First course?
4 The name of your class tutor, group tutor or personal tutor (if different from 3).

Your fellow students

One of the distinctive features of BTEC courses is the amount of group work when working with other students. So, to make your course as worthwhile and enjoyable as possible you need to get to know the other students in your class. It takes effort to get to know people, but once you have done so you will find it is valuable. Indeed, one of the common skills is working with others and if you know and like the people you are working with, you will work better in groups. One of the main points employers look for when they are recruiting people is the ability to get on with others.

ACTIVITY

In order to get to know your fellow students:

1 Pair up with a student who you do not know already.
2 Find out and write down the following information about that person:

- name
- hobbies and interests
- work experience
- if he/she has a job
- if he/she has a job what is it and what does it involve?
- what does he/she consider to be his/her six top strengths which will help him/her to be successful in the course?

3 You and your partner should now pair up with another pair who you do not know. Each person in turn should introduce their partner to the other two students and tell them the information learnt about their partner.

Assessing yourself

You know about the centre and your course. What about yourself? What do you know about your own strengths and weaknesses? You are going to take stock of yourself. We all think we know ourselves but it can help to sit down and take time to think about ourselves, including our strengths and weaknesses and how other people see us – sometimes they can see strengths and weaknesses in us that we did not know existed.

ACTIVITY

Read the list of words below and pick out the 'I am' words and the 'I would like to be' words (those which describe what you would like to be). You may add additional words to the list if you wish. An example is included:

I AM	I WOULD LIKE TO BE
Good at talking	Able to listen

Kind, punctual, reliable, well-mannered, able to listen, hard-working, trustworthy, good at spelling, conscientious, able to concentrate, good at calculations, responsible, able to work on my own, able to use a computer, likeable, good at working with others, able to make friends easily, helpful to others, able to learn things quickly, good at talking, good at listening.

Many of the things that you are good at on your list will be a result of having had the chance to gain experience. If you are not good at something it may be because you have not had the chance yet. It is therefore useful to assess your experience and highlight where you need to get more experience during the course.

ACTIVITY

List all the clerical tasks you have done either at work, while on work experience, in a part-time job or in school. Then next to each of the clerical tasks you have listed indicate your experience of the task. An example is included.

COMPETENCE	EXPERIENCE	DETAILS OF EXPERIENCE
Filing	Part-time job	I work for Carson's on Saturday and do some filing for them.
	Placement from school	I spent three weeks at Barclays and did some filing there.
	School	We did filing in GCSE business studies.

Now complete the same exercise for each of the clerical tasks you have not experienced (use list on pp14–15).

Action plans

Now you have thought about yourself and how other people see you it would be useful for you to make a personal action plan. This involves setting goals for yourself, identifying things you want to learn and what you want to improve, and planning ahead. A typical action plan for a BTEC First student might be like the one shown in the following activity.

Complete the personal action plan for yourself and discuss it with your tutor.

Personal Action Plan

Name: ....

Long term

1 My goals for the next three years are:

2 I will be helped to achieve these goals by:

3 I may have problems achieving these goals because:

4 In order to try and achieve these goals I need to do the following:

What I need to do	By when	How

Short term

1 My goals for the next three months are:

2 I will be helped to achieve these goals by:

3 I may have problems achieving these goals because:

4 In order to try and achieve these goals I need to do the following:

What I need to do   *By when*   *How*

Other things I need to improve

Fig 3.1 A personal action plan form

Learning and studying skills

Perhaps you think that after many years of school you know how to study and learn. Unfortunately many people have poor study skills when it comes to learning for themselves rather than remembering what they are told; and even the people who have quite good study skills can always do with improvement. It is especially important to have good skills in:

1 listening   2 note taking
3 reading   4 planning.

1 Listening

Listening skills are important for your success not only on your course but also at work. While on your course you will need to listen to talks given by centre staff, visiting speakers and employers. You need to be able to listen to instructions so that you know how to do certain tasks. You may need to listen to videos and while doing group work you need to be able to listen to your peers. At work you need to listen to instructions from your supervisor, requests from customers and clients, and people when they introduce themselves.

2 Note taking

Note taking skills are required for learning – taking notes of instructions, information, etc. They are also skills required for effective communication. Communicating is one of the common skills considered in Unit 2 and is vital for a number of clerical tasks:

- taking and leaving messages
- keeping notes of instructions
- taking notes in a meeting
- recording instructions.

3 Reading for learning

This skill is important because much information is passed on in written form, e.g.:

- training manuals
- induction manuals
- instruction booklets
- product specifications
- sales literature
- textbooks and workbooks.

Sometimes you can read something without having learnt from it.

4 Planning your assignment work

This is a very necessary skill because you need to be able to:

- meet deadlines
- organise your work
- present your work.

Some of the clerical tasks which you need to acquire have what is known as **time constraints** – which means that tasks have to be carried out within a set time. If you take longer then you will not be considered to be competent. As you can imagine, an employer is concerned with speed and efficiency as well as accuracy – in a business *time costs money*.

Tips to improve your study skills

Listening skills

Let nothing make your mind wander, e.g. your weekend activities.
If you find your mind wandering try again and do not give up.
Shut out distractions caused by noise by concentrating on what is being said.
Tell the speaker if you do not understand. Lack of understanding will cause you not to listen and you will switch off.
Enjoy the topics being taught, make yourself interested in them and you will find the talk interesting – just think of your future success.
Note taking helps you to listen by keeping you interested and alert.

Note taking

Note main heading next to the margin and indent sub headings – using headings gives structure to your notes.
Organise your notes by numbering and lettering.
Take a new line for each point. Do not cram too much into one space.
Errors should not be erased because it takes up time and you may miss important information. Just draw a single line through the error.
Telephone messages should be written down. Do not forget to ask the caller for their name and number and read this and the message back to the caller to ensure you have heard correctly.
A badly written, illegible note is no use to anyone.
Keep your notes neat so that you can read them later.
If the speaker says that something is important write it down and mark it with an asterisk, a circle or a box. If you miss something, leave a space and copy it later.
Notes of lessons are only useful if you can find them easily when you want them – make sure that they are filed well so that you can refer to them when you want to.
Get the meaning of the message or what is being said rather than the exact words, except in cases where the exact words are very important.

Reading for learning

Ready to read – you need pencils, pens and paper so that you can make notes of the main points as you go along.
Ensure that you have a comfortable chair and enough light.

A brief scanning of the content will give you an overview of the material.

Do read carefully – word by word where you are learning something new.

Improve your understanding of what you are reading by reading confusing parts more than once. If they still do not make sense to you leave them for now.

Notes which you have made should be read over to help you remember them.

Go back to parts which you may have left because they were difficult.

Planning your assignment work

All assignments will have a deadline – make sure that you know when it is and plan to get the work done before it. Leave time for correcting errors and mistakes.

Spelling and punctuation are important – reading over work before you hand it on can save you from some simple errors.

Simple things like a cover, a contents page, dividers for sections and a clear layout make work far easier to read and use.

In completing an assignment you are proving that you are competent – look at the work that you are going to hand in – is that what it says about you?

Get all the information you need before you start the assignment – it is easier to have too much information and cut it down than to have to work something in later or miss it out.

No one is impressed by a lot of paper for paper's sake and you will not get a better mark for a thick assignment than a thin one if the work is better in the thin one.

Most assignments are based on the tasks that you would have to do at work; so think about work, ask people who do a job and look at textbooks before you do the assignment.

Each assignment counts towards the competences that you need. Do not think that you can do badly on one and make it up on another – you will have to do it right in the future, so why not now?

Not all assignments require written work – when you have a practical task to do make sure that you keep copies of the work covered as proof of your competence in the task.

Time is valuable. When you have an assignment you need to make sure that you have planned the time properly. If you spend too little time on something you will not succeed as well as you could. If you spend too much time you will be short of time for other work.

Some of the questions in this activity will be to help you to remember information about the BTEC First course which you learnt earlier. If you have forgotten any of this information then look back. Question 14 should only be completed by full-time students.

1 What are 'common skills'?
2 List the seven common skills on your BTEC First course.
3 Explain what 'work role' is.
4 List six of the clerical tasks which form part of your core:
5 What option units are offered by the centre?
6 How many option units should you take?
7 What are assignments?
8 How many assignments will you be required to do on the course?
9 Will you be working in a training office for any time during the course? If so, where is it, and what sort of work does it do?
10 Have you got an outline of the work that you will be doing during the year and which topics you will be covering when? If not, ask if you can have one.
11 Are there any trips, residential courses or days out that you need to know about? If there are, will they cost anything? How much?
12 What are 'competencies'?
13 What are your course dates?
14 How long is your work experience and when is it?

Summary

1 *At the beginning of your BTEC First course you will have an induction to introduce you to the centre where you are studying. You will learn about the facilities at the centre, the staff who will be teaching you, health and safety and other regulations and details of your course.*

2 *Get to know your fellow students as soon as possible so you can settle into your course quickly and work well in groups.*

3 *Learn about yourself, your strengths, your weaknesses, your experiences and make an Action Plan to help you improve your skills.*

4 *Some of the study skills you will need on the course are listening, note taking, reading and planning. These skills are vital for success on your BTEC First course and at work.*

This set of units aims to:

- *Develop your knowledge of clerical tasks.*
- *Provide you with a chance to practise some of the main tasks.*
- *Explain the importance of these clerical tasks in a busy office.*

Business support systems

Although every clerical job is different, employers and the National Council for Vocational Qualifications (NCVQ) have decided there are a number of very specific clerical competences which anyone working in administration or in a clerical job must have. Each of these clerical competences is covered in a separate unit in this section of the book. However, to be considered fully competent you may have to show a competency several times over an extended period of time or in different circumstances. Just working through the unit alone is not enough to make you competent. For each clerical competence the unit provides an explanation of the background knowledge needed and some activities or tasks to help you to develop your competence. In a real office though, work may involve using a number of different competences simultaneously in dealing with a task. Unit 14, therefore, includes a number of assignments which are longer and more complex than the activities in Units 4 to 13 and involve a number of competences as well as the Common Skills you looked at in Part A.

HEALTH AND SAFETY

This unit aims to:

- *Identify the consequences of accidents at work.*
- *Explain the laws and rules which aim to protect people at work.*
- *Identify safety hazards in offices and ways to avoid them.*
- *Encourage you to find out about procedures for reporting accidents and fires in your place of work or your work experience placement.*
- *Encourage you to find out about fire drills.*

4

Being at work can seriously damage your health. Most people know someone who has suffered an injury at work. Most people at work have had a lucky escape at some time or another. So everyone at work needs to think about health and safety and to take as much care as they can because:

- Accidents at work can injure people badly and ruin their lives.
- Accidents and injuries mean people have time off work and this can be costly to an employer.
- Employers are forced by law to keep to health and safety rules and can end up in court if the rules are not followed by their employees – so can the employee who breaks the health and safety rules.

Health and safety is so important that there are laws to protect people at work such as the:

- Health and Safety at Work Act (1974)
- Offices, Shops and Railway Premises Act (1963)
- Fire Precautions Act (1971).

The main piece of law, however, is the Health and Safety at Work Act (1974) which places responsibility for health and safety on both the employer and the employee:

1 *The employer* needs to ensure that the workplace is safe in general and that employees have appropriate training to use equipment and knowledge in health and safety.
2 *The employee* is responsible for: keeping to the health and safety rules

'What do you mean 'incompetent fool'? I got 85 per cent at school for my essay on health and safety.'

set by their employer; not tampering with equipment which is provided for their safety and the safety of others; and not doing anything which might cause damage to themselves and others.

Health and safety in the office

It is easy to think of hazards in restaurant kitchens, on building sites or on the shop floor, but there are hazards in offices too. Some typical accidents which have happened in offices are given below.

Janet *We took turns at going to the vending machine for coffee and crisps. We always took a box to carry the drinks in. One day it was my turn and I was wearing a big baggy woollen jumper. My jumper got caught in the door handle while I was carrying the box of hot drinks. The hot drinks flew over me and I got burnt.*

Olga *I slipped on some water which had been spilt in the corridor. I hurt myself badly. It was likely that someone had fetched some water to water the plants and spilt some or it could have been that someone spilt a drink.*

Richard *I was moving a computer from one room to another. The computer was very light. I held onto the computer and turned to open the door and as I turned I put my back out. I was off work for weeks and was unable to move.*

Jasmin *Someone left the bottom drawer of a filing cabinet open. I wasn't looking where I was going and tripped over it. My leg was badly bruised.*

Jeff *There was a bit of worn carpet near my desk and I sometimes used to catch my heel on it. Then one day I caught my heel in it and fell against my desk. I was carrying three heavy box files at the time. They went flying, hitting the person next to me and I was badly hurt too.*

Make a note of the hazards that the people above experienced and, next to them, suggest how these hazards could have been avoided. Jasmin's experience is given as an example.

ACTIVITY

HAZARD	COULD HAVE BEEN AVOIDED BY
Filing cabinet open	Stickers on cabinets warning people to close drawers when not in use. Training to warn people of the risk and to remind people to close cabinets and to watch for open ones

There are many other common hazards too, including the following:

- Smoking
- Trailing cables
- Machinery
- Lifting heavy equipment incorrectly
- Blocked fire doors
- Fire doors held open
- Touching electrical switches with wet hands
- Handbags on the floor
- Feet sticking out into the aisles
- Incorrect posture for sitting
- Poorly lit rooms and corridors
- Rushing around

You will probably find examples of all of these, and more, in any office that you enter.

For each of the hazards listed above note the damage that could occur from it. Smoking is used as an example.

ACTIVITY

HAZARD	DAMAGE
Smoking	Fire Cancer 'Passive smoking' for non-smokers in the office

There are some tips below to help you to remember ways to keep safe. They are not complex and might seem like common sense, but they are important, and they could save you or someone else from an accident.

House safety rules
- Use your head to foresee hazards.
- Report health and safety hazards such as worn carpets, loose tiles, lights not working and faulty equipment.
- Do not use equipment that you have not been trained to use.
- Use equipment correctly.
- Be alert.
- Get to know the firm's safety rules and regulations and follow them at all times.

Reporting accidents

Accidents at work should always be reported and there will be a set procedure for doing this. It is important that even small accidents are reported for a number of reasons:

- It is the law that the employer has to keep a record of accidents.
- If you do not report an accident, a hazard may get worse and someone may be badly injured in the future – by reporting a minor hazard it can be fixed quickly and easily.
- A small injury now might be more serious later and the employer will need proof of what happened, as will the person hurt.
- A clear record of all accidents allows employers to see if there is a pattern and to provide training if there is a need.

ACTIVITY

Find out the following for your place of work, your work experience placement or the centre where you are doing the course.

1 If you have an accident who should you report it to?
2 Is there a special accident form which you would need to complete?
3 Who would you give the completed form to, and what will happen to it?
4 Is there an accident book for recording accidents?
5 Where is the book kept, and who checks it?
6 Who are the first aiders and where would you find them?
7 Where are the first aid boxes kept? What is in them?

Fires

A fire at work is potentially the most serious health and safety hazard because it can spread quickly through a building and badly damage people and equipment. A big fire can put a firm out of business if they lose all their records, equipment, premises, etc.

It is important to find out the procedures for reporting fires and what you should do in the event of a fire. There will be notices in the building showing the way to fire escapes, explaining what to do if you find a fire and showing you where alarms and extinguishers are kept. You should also have regular practices and be trained on what to do in the event of a fire when you start in a new job or a new college.

ACTIVITY

Find out the following for your place of work, your work experience placement or the centre where you are doing your course.

1 What does the fire alarm sound like? Are there any other alarm signals that you might hear – for a bomb alert perhaps? What are they like?

2 Where are the fire escape routes and where do you assemble when you are out of the building?

3 Are there any special rules that you have to follow on your way out, such as switching off machines?

4 How do you report a fire if you discover one?

5 Where are the fire extinguishers kept? Are there special ones for use on different types of fires? Do you know how to use them and which ones to use when?

There are a few rules that you should always remember (*see* Fig 4.1).

FIRE/EVACUATION PROCEDURE

Instructions to staff

Action to be taken in case of fire or other emergency

Assembly point: **FRONT CAR PARK**

If you discover a fire:

1 Immediately operate the nearest fire alarm call point

2 Attack the fire, if possible, with the appliances provided but without taking personal risks – ensuring a clear escape route is available at all times

On hearing the fire alarm:

3 The Receptionist on duty will call the Fire Brigade immediately.

4 Leave the building and report to the person in charge of the assembly point at the place indicated above, where a roll call will be taken

5 The senior person or authorised deputy on the affected floor will take charge of any evacuation and ensure that no one is left in the area

- USE THE NEAREST AVAILABLE EXIT

- DO NOT USE THE LIFT
(unless specifically provided and indicated as a means of escape for persons with disabilities)

- DO NOT STOP TO COLLECT PERSONAL BELONGINGS

- DO NOT RUN OR PANIC

- IF YOU HAVE VISITORS ESCORT THEM TO THE ASSEMBLY POINT

- DO NOT RE-ENTER THE BUILDING FOR ANY REASON UNTIL THE SAFETY OFFICER GIVES YOU PERMISSION

(Notice for display in premises having a simple alarm system – to be displayed on notice boards, in all rooms and by each fire alarm point)

Fig 4.1 A standard fire notice

Summary

1 Accidents at work can injure people badly, cause staff absenteeism and can cost an employer a great deal of money in compensation claims.

2 Employers are forced by law to keep to health and safety rules and can end up in court if the rules are broken by them or their employees.

3 Some important laws which set health and safety standards and protect people at work are:
- Health and Safety at Work Act
- Offices, Shops and Railway Premises Act
- Fire Precautions Act.

4 The Health and Safety at Work Act places responsibility for health and safety on both the employer and the employee.

5 There are many health and safety hazards in offices.

6 Health and safety hazards can be avoided in many ways such as by being careful, considerate and alert, and not using equipment without having had adequate training.

7 Always report health and safety hazards.

8 Always report accidents even a small accident. An accident which seems minor at the time it happened can worsen with time.

9 Fire at work can damage both people and equipment. Do not smoke in places where there are 'no smoking' signs, learn the fire rules and follow them at all times.

10 Find out what you should do in the event of a fire and make yourself familiar with fire escapes, fire alarms and where fire extinguishers are kept. Take part in fire practices.

GETTING ORGANISED – FILING

This unit aims to:

- *Explain the need for filing.*
- *Explain how to file documents.*
- *Explain how files are stored.*
- *Develop your competency in filing.*

5

This unit is about one of the most basic clerical skills – being able to file paper and extract information from files when required.

'I'm sorry, but the file is not available.'

The illustration shows something that must never happen. It is important to learn how to file so that you will not waste the firm's money and your own time by being disorganised. Businesses have numerous documents to keep in good order, to keep clean and safe such as letters, bank statements, invoices and order forms. Such important documents are needed for future reference. For example, the VAT inspectors inspect financial records of firms – they look at invoices, order forms and other financial records. Every department in an organisation will keep records of some kind which must be filed for future reference. In this section you will learn how to do basic filing and you will find further practice in the assignments. You can also practise by filing all your course notes, copies of letters you send to firms and so on. Organising your own paperwork will help you to organise paperwork in business.

ACTIVITY

Choose three departments in a firm and identify documents and records which are stored by each one. An example is included.

DEPARTMENT	RECORDS KEPT
Reception	Visitors in and out book
	Logs of phone calls
	Diary of visitors expected
	Names and locations of staff

How to file

You can file documents by the following methods:

Name **(alphabetical filing)**	Company names, names of people – just like the telephone directory
Number **(numerical filing)**	Invoices, order forms, petty cash vouchers, library books
Subject **(subject filing)**	Car, gas, telephone, etc. – the subjects are normally filed in alphabetical order. You can arrange your BTEC First file in subject order.
Location **(geographical filing)**	Town, county, country – the locations are then filed in alphabetical order.
Date **(chronological order)**	Date order – normally used for arranging documents within files, e.g. the subject could be 'gas' and

	all the gas bills could be stored in date order.
Combination of letters and numbers (alphanumerical filing)	First by name, then by number

These are the rules

Alphabetical filing

RULES	EXAMPLES
Filing people	
1 Use the person's surname first; if the name is double-barrelled ignore the hyphen	Fox, Green, Smythe
2 Where several people have the same surname use the first name; where people have identical names use the town	Fox, Amanda; Fox, Simon
3 Put short before long	Shortt, D; Shortt, Damian
4 Mc, M' and Mac treated as Mac	MacBride, McDonald
5 Saint and St treated as Saint	
6 Treat prefixes like O, de and Van as part of the name	O'Donald, Van Berlo
7 Ignore titles, e.g. Mr, Mrs, Lady	
Filing firms	
1 Some names of firms are names of people and the rules above should be followed when filing	John Smith Ltd – file under Smith John Ltd
2 If the name of the firm is not the name of a person, then take each word in turn ignoring words like a, an, of, the and in	The Chocolate Box – file under Chocolate Box

3 Disregard apostrophes, hyphens and ampersands

4 If there is a number in the name treat it as if it were spelt in full

7th Heaven – file under Seventh Heaven

5 If the firm has initials which are known file as if they were written in full

AA – file under Automobile Association

6 If the name of the firm has initials which are not known they are filed before the names of firms written in full

MNG Whittingtons
Millingtons Ltd

Numerical filing

RULES	EXAMPLE
This is easy – you just file documents in the order of the number, the lower number before the higher	123, 124, 125, 126

1 Put the following client names in alphabetical order: Mark Bedford, Stephen O'Donald, Mary Shepherd, Amanda MacKenna, Angela Kay, Mini Rutherglen, Susan McDermott, Helen Keenan, Michael O'Grady, Nicola Summers, Elsie Duck, Marjorie Soley

2 Put the following dates in chronological order. 5–8–1991, 5 Aug 1989, 6 Sept 1990, 8–1–90, 17–09–90, 30–09–90, 18 February 1991, 30 May 1990

3 Put the following invoice numbers in numerical order.

Invoice no 0103589	Invoice no 1907485
0107589	38719089
010584	570398
1345990	0982478

Learning filing for the first time – your questions answered?

Question   What do I do when I am asked to file a batch of documents?
Answer   This is what to do

1 Collect all the documents together being careful not to drop any.

2 Pre-sort the documents and check they have been dealt with and are ready to be filed. This can be indicated by a special mark, e.g. F, FILE or a stamp saying FILE. A mark or symbol like this is a **release symbol** and documents which have the symbol are said to have been **released for filing**, that is, they have been dealt with and can now be filed away for future reference.

3 Identify the name under which the document is to be filed and mark it (this is called the **filing point**, **caption** or **title**).

4 Replace paper clips with staples.

5 Sort the documents into batches, e.g. put all documents from the same firm together to save time.

6 File the documents placing the most recent paper at the front of the file or on top of the other papers in the file.

Much of this can be done at the same time – for example you can: check that the document has been released for filing; staple the documents clipped together with paper clips; and identify the filing point.

Question   What happens if I am in charge of files and someone wants to take a file out?

Answer   There may be a book for the borrower to sign stating the borrower's name, department, file and date borrowed. When the file is given back the date of return is noted. If there is no book you should make a note of who has the file in a safe place and cross it off the list of 'files out' when it comes back.

Question   What happens if someone wants to take a document out of a file?

Answer   An **out card** is put into the file to replace the paper. It will detail the borrower's name, department, file and date borrowed. When the document is returned the date is noted.

Question   What happens if I do not know where to file a document or am unable to find a document?

Answer   You should ask a more experienced member of staff or your supervisor.

Question   What about confidential files?

Answer   Some files are confidential and only certain people can have access to them. Organisations tend to have their own rules relating to confidential files and documents.

Question   What do I do if I have documents and there are no files open, e.g. for a firm which we have not dealt with before?

Answer   You can put the documents in the file marked **miscellaneous**, but once there are a few documents with the same title then you should open a file specially for those documents.

Question I have heard clerks talking about **cross referencing**. What does this mean?

Answer Sometimes there may be more than one filing point for a document. Each of the filing points which are not used will have a cross reference sheet or card inserted in them to tell you where to look for the file (*see* Fig 5.1). You may have seen cross referencing in the *Yellow Pages* when you have looked for one category and there is a note telling you to look under another heading in the book.

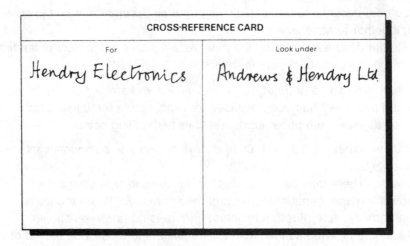

Fig 5.1 A cross-reference card

ACTIVITY

Answer the questions below from the information that you have been given in the unit.

1 What do the following words mean?

- Release symbols
- Filing point
- Miscellaneous
- Cross reference

2 What is an out card and why is it used?

3 Why are paper clips replaced with staples when pre-sorting documents.

4 Why are there different methods of filing?

Indexing

Many books have an **index** to enable readers to find information quickly without having to look through the whole book. You will probably have a phone book or an address book which is indexed alphabetically so that you can look up phone numbers and addresses of people quickly. If you want to know the address of Billy Runshaw you will look up 'R'. Offices also use index systems (indexed books or card indexes) for telephone numbers, addresses, business cards or other information which is needed. Where a numerical filing system is used there is normally an alphabetical index showing the names for each number.

Where are the files kept?

There are many types of file ranging from suspension files (*see* Fig 5.2) to ringbinders which you may use for your BTEC First coursework notes. The most common way of keeping large numbers of files is in filing cabinets with a number of drawers in them – usually between two and four. The files are stored one behind the other in the drawers. This is known as a vertical filing system.

Fig 5.2 Suspension files

Another way of keeping large numbers of files is in a filing cupboard where the files are stored next to each other. This is known as a lateral filing system.

Although in most firms there are manual filing systems, many firms both large and small store information on computers. These files which are held on computer are accessed and updated just as a manual system would be. There are many advantages of information being stored on computers but many firms still find it necessary to keep manual files and some firms use both systems. The following comments give an indication of why different businesses use computers for filing.

- We need to store so much information that computers save us space.
- It is much faster for us, we do not need to leave the desk to find a file.
- Well it is more up to date, isn't it?
- We can use passwords so that only certain people can access the files.

Below are some comments about why manual systems are used.

- We find it faster because we do not keep a lot of records.
- We wouldn't know what programmes to use or how to work them.
- We would need a very complex system and I don't know what is available.
- It would cost too much to buy a computer.
- In many cases it is easier to have manual files.
- We store invoices and receipts, etc. which we are sent – we need to keep these manually.

Summary

1 *Good filing allows a business to keep documents in good order and safe and allows them to be found quickly when they are needed.*

2 *Documents can be filed alphabetically, numerically, geographically, by subject, by chronological order or alphanumerically.*

3 *Although there are basic rules for filing, organisations can have their own individual systems and rules.*

4 *Indexing enables you to find information quickly.*

5 *There are many pieces of equipment used in filing, ranging from different types of files to filing cabinets, cupboards and computers.*

6 *Many firms store files on computers.*

7 *Although computers are popular for storing files manual systems are still used, in large and small firms.*

8 *Some reasons for using computers to store files are that less space is needed, it can save time, it can be convenient, and more secure than manual systems.*

9 *Some advantages of a manual system for storing records are that it can be fast if few records are kept, it is easy, and computers can cost more than manual systems.*

BUSINESS COMMUNICATIONS

This unit aims to:

- *Explain the importance of having good telephone skills.*
- *Show you how to make and accept telephone calls.*
- *Show you how to take telephone messages.*
- *Explain how you can deal with callers face-to-face.*
- *Develop your competency in business communications.*

This unit is about the main forms of written and spoken communication in business.

Telephone and face to face communication

Telephone skills and face to face communication need similar skills. The difference is that when the telephone is used customers and clients cannot see your face and therefore the sound of your voice is very important to make the customer or client feel comfortable. In face to face communications the customer or client sees all of you and therefore everything about you is important – even if you say nothing your body tells tales.

The importance of the phone

The telephone is widely used in business. For example, it is used to make enquiries, confirm arrangements, sell and carry out market research. Many people worry about answering the phone when they first start work. In the story below Nazma tells of her experience when she just started work.

Nazma   *I was employed as an office junior in the wages department and at first I didn't need to answer the phone. But soon I was given the responsibility of wages for a number of employees. The wages were paid on a Thursday which meant that on Fridays you were bombarded with calls from staff enquiring about their wages. It all seemed so complicated and I didn't know all the words they used or how to look up the tables quickly. With being new I was inexperienced and slow. The other clerks dealt with the queries so well I was worried about showing myself up. I was so embarrassed when the phone rang. It felt as if everyone was listening to me making a fool of myself. It seems so silly because it's the part of the job I enjoy most now.*

Nazma was afraid because she worried about being asked questions which she could not answer and people around her hearing her conversation. These are common worries but once you have answered the phone a few times at work you get used to it. Remember that you can always ask someone in the office for any information which you are not sure about. Also do not forget that the people around you are not listening to you – they have their own work to do and they are not really interested in your conversation.

Answering the phone

Make sure that you are always prepared to answer the telephone by having some writing paper or a telephone message pad and something to write with. It is important to keep all your files as up to date as possible so that you can deal with queries quickly. You need to be familiar with where and how information is stored and with the office filing system so that you can find files quickly.

Some telephone systems can be complex and it is important to get to know the equipment – many of the facilities that a modern phone system offers can make your life easier, for example:

- **Memories** allow you to call numbers that are used frequently just by pressing a couple of buttons.
- **Redial buttons** allow you to try a number again if you have called and not been able to get through.
- **Secrecy, silence** or **mute buttons** allow you to talk to other people in the office without the caller being able to hear you. Remember that putting your hand over the mouthpiece does not stop the person on the other end of the phone hearing what you are saying.
- **Hands-free dialling** allows you to call a number without lifting the handset until the person answers. Some systems allow you to carry on a conversation without having to lift the handset at all – so you can keep your hands free to take notes or use a calculator.
- **Conference calls** allow you to talk to up to three other people at the same time – a sort of mini conference.
- **Fax**, a method of sending documents to another office down the phone lines, allows you to send important documents to anyone who has a fax receiver in a matter of a few seconds.

If your office phone works on a switchboard you will probably also be able to:

- get an outside line
- transfer calls to another extension
- transfer calls back to the switchboard.

Dealing with the call

The flow-chart illustrated identifies important stages to follow when answering the phone. The main stages shown on the chart are briefly explained overleaf.

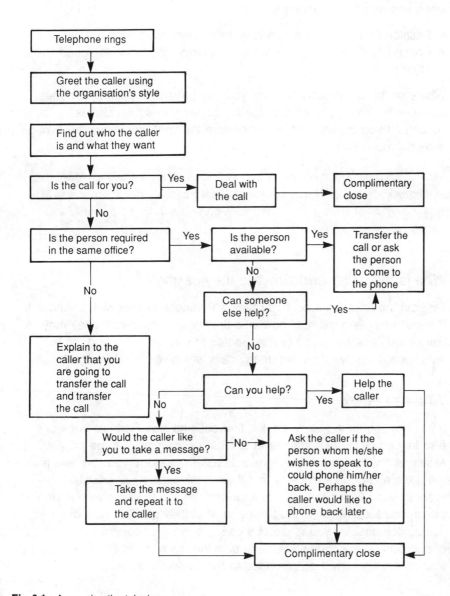

Fig 6.1 Answering the telephone

Telephone rings

Many firms tell their staff not to answer the phone immediately when it rings. They advise staff to let the phone ring a few times because this enables callers to collect their thoughts if they have not prepared themselves for the call.

Greeting the caller

Many firms have a house style which they train members of staff to use when answering the telephone, e.g:

- Fashion Footwear Limited, this is Julie speaking, how may I help you?
- Brown and Coopers Chartered Accountants, good morning/good afternoon.

Whatever the organisational style, you need to sound polite, courteous and friendly. When you answer the phone, as far as the caller is concerned *you are the firm*, and therefore the firm's reputation and image rests on you.

ACTIVITY

What is the organisational style? When you make calls over the next few weeks write down how the employee answered. What was the organisational style in each case? What image did you get of the organisation from the people who answered your calls?

Who is the caller and why are they calling?

Find out the caller's name, what they want and who they wish to speak to. Sometimes callers will not know who they wish to speak to. They may have been directed to you or misdirected to you, or if you work on the switchboard you will deal with many calls which you need to direct.

Who can help?

If you are unable to help the caller find out who can. Perhaps someone else in your office, or someone in another department, can be of assistance. If there is no one available ask the caller if you can take a message and get someone to ring them back as soon as possible. In order to know who can help it is important for you to know 'who is who' in the organisation, who the staff are and what they do. This type of information enables you to direct a caller to the right person or department. Many companies have directories which list employees and their extension numbers. You need to learn how to use this.

Transferring the call

It is important to find out how to transfer calls to another extension and back to the switchboard.

Taking a message and passing it on

If the caller would like you to take a message, write the message down straight away and repeat the message to the caller to make sure it is correct. Sometimes people leave a message but forget to give their name. It is better if you find out the name of the caller at the beginning of the call and then you will be able to use their name during the conversation.

Often there are special pads containing message forms which look like the one illustrated in Fig 6.2.

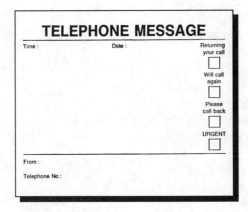

Fig 6.2   Example of a telephone message form

Sometimes when you are taking a message you cannot hear the caller clearly. Use the **telephone alphabet** to help with clarifying spellings of, for example, the caller's name and address.

The telephone alphabet

A	Alfred	K	King	U	Uncle
B	Benjamin	L	London	V	Victor
C	Charlie	M	Mary	W	William
D	David	N	Nellie	X	X-Ray
E	Edward	O	Oliver	Y	Yellow
F	Frederick	P	Peter	Z	Zebra
G	George	Q	Queen		
H	Harry	R	Robert		
I	Isaac	S	Samuel		
J	Jack	T	Tommy		

Pass the message on as soon as possible. The firm could lose business if calls are not taken.

ACTIVITY

Look at the messages below and make a note of what is wrong with each of them. What information should the person taking the message have made sure is noted down?

MESSAGE	WHAT IS MISSING
Alan, Peter phoned and asked you to call him back about Friday. Jo.	Date Time Which Peter? Phone number?
14–9, 3.45 Jo, Peter Smith called to speak to you. He'll call back later.	
16–10 Anita – Mr Harper called and asked if you can phone him back in an hour's time Narendra	
Wednesday 15th, 2.20pm Brian, Carl Benson would like you to phone him on 34098. He was returning your call. Alan	

Giving a good image

Throughout the call it is important to get on well with the customer or client. You can do this by being friendly and courteous. Do not forget that when you are using the telephone it is only your voice that the customer hears – they cannot see your facial expression. Your voice must sound good. Some firms tell their staff to *smile* when they are using the phone since this smile should make you feel better and your voice will sound friendlier – these firms use the slogan *smile then dial* and it applies both to making calls and answering calls.

Confirming arrangements

You need to be familiar with confirmation procedures. Does the firm like the client/customer to confirm an order by completing and sending an order form, or will a letter do? If it is an internal call, for example, you may be taking a booking for refreshments to be provided at a meeting – do you need this in writing?

Confidential information

There is often information which is confidential and should not be disclosed under any circumstances. This type of information will differ depending on the organisation but normally addresses and home telephone numbers of staff, customers and clients are not disclosed. Financial information and personnel matters are usually confidential and information stored on computers is subject to special rules under the Data Protection Act which is dealt with in more detail in Unit 7.

During the call

Ask questions to find out who the caller is, what he/she wants, and any other relevant information. Listen to the replies from the caller as well as their requests. There must be no distractions hindering you from listening. Find information for the caller from other employees if you are unsure about something and look up information from directories or sales literature if necessary. If, however, your enquiries are likely to take a long time, then politely tell the caller that you will find out the details and call back. While the caller is speaking you can write down the relevant information.

Ask the caller their name so that you can refer to it, making a note of what the caller wants. This saves you asking the caller to repeat information and is also helpful if you need to transfer the call since you will be able to tell the third party who the caller is and what they want. This saves the caller the frustration of having to repeat everything again.

Speak clearly – the caller cannot see your mouth move as they would be able to in face to face communication. It is therefore important for you to move your mouth pronouncing words clearly. If you cannot be understood when giving information such as spelling names and addresses use the telephone alphabet to help you.

One point to remember is that the caller can hear everything you say – even if you are speaking to a colleague rather than into the phone or have your hand over the mouthpiece. So if you need to say something that you do not want the caller to hear use the silence or mute button on the phone to make sure that they cannot hear you.

Time to go

An important skill is to end the call without it appearing abrupt. Sometimes it may seem as though a caller wishes to speak forever but you should practise ending the conversation politely and in a friendly manner. This is also important for face to face communications. One technique used to end calls is to summarise what is going to be done as a result of the call, e.g:

- So I will check if the order can be delivered tomorrow and ring you back straight away if there is a problem.
- I'll tell John you rang and pass the message on to him as soon as he comes in.
- I will tell him that it is urgent and he will ring you back straight away.

Ending the call is also important because it can leave a lasting impression in the caller's mind. You should thank the customer/client for calling. Even if the caller was making a complaint you should thank them for bringing it to your attention.

Making calls

Most jobs involve making telephone calls. You may be asked to make a call for a customer or client, e.g. a client may wish you to call for a taxi. The section above on answering the phone is applicable here but in addition you should:

1 Make sure the call is necessary – before making a call always ask yourself if it is needed. Calls cost money. If it is important can the call be made when the rate is cheaper? Imagine a map with zones coloured red, yellow and green. Green is the local zone where calls are relatively inexpensive, the yellow zone is further away from your firm and if you must make calls in this zone use the cheap rate time if possible. The red zone is the stop zone – do not phone that zone unless in emergency situations – write instead.

Find out how far each of the call areas goes and what it costs to make a call in each of them. Use the headings below under which to set out your findings:

AREA	DISTANCE	COST

2 Use directories to find unknown numbers. There may be some special directories that you will have to use but the most common ones are:

- Local phone book
- *Yellow Pages*
- *Thomson's Local*
- Industrial and commercial *Yellow Pages*.

Directory Enquiries will try to find a number for you if you are unable to get it from a directory and they also have an international directory service to help you find numbers in other countries. However, BT does charge for this.

3 Plan your call. You may find making notes beforehand useful as a memory jogger.

4 Check the number and dial carefully. If you dial the wrong number you are costing your firm unnecessary money. You will need to write the number down if someone tells you a number, e.g. a client or directory enquiries giving you a number.

5 Sometimes your switchboard operator will ask the purpose of the call. This is done to ensure that calls made are business calls and not personal calls. You should be able to explain the reason for the call to the operator.

6 Leave a message on an answering machine if there is one so that the person who is contacting can call you back. This saves you time and the firm money.

7 Report faulty equipment as soon as possible and give as much detail as you can. It is helpful to indicate what is wrong: 'I can't hear people properly on this phone – there's a crackling noise on the line – but it doesn't happen on the other phones in the office'.

8 Always keep a list of emergency numbers such as hospital, police and first aider, in case you are faced with an emergency situation.

Face to face business

Unlike when you use the phone the caller can see you face to face. This has certain implications because your body talks. It means that you have to be suitably dressed and need to be aware of how you stand, your facial expressions and any gestures that you make – they all convey an impression and say things about you and your firm. This section will deal specifically with this and how to make the caller welcome.

Making the caller welcome

Do not keep the caller waiting, acknowledge their presence straight away and make them feel welcome.

Read the experience of Susan, a sales representative, and explain how she could be made to feel more welcome by the firms she is complaining about.

Susan My job was to sell computer paper to firms in the London area. I liked the products I sold because they were good quality. The part of the job I didn't like was the way that I was sometimes treated by reception staff. Some were really great and made you feel good but in some companies I could mention they were really awful. They kept you waiting while they seemed to be phoning their friends, and if I had to wait to see someone even when I had an appointment some of them never apologised. I mean, it's basic manners isn't it? They could have said something like 'I'm sorry to keep you waiting but . . .' It doesn't hurt to be polite. Some of the reception staff sometimes give you the impression that they think they are better than you because you are 'just a Rep'. They don't need to say anything – it just shows.

How could Susan have been made to feel more welcome?

You can make a caller feel welcome by:

- the surroundings
- your greeting and acknowledgment
- your smile
- your manner
- your dress
- being helpful.

It is also easy to make visitors feel that you are not bothered or that you do not want to see them. Try to make sure that you give the right impression.

How your body talks

Can you normally tell if someone likes or dislikes you, is pleased to see you or not, is interested in what you say or is confused, bored or in a hurry even if that person does not say anything? Often this is possible because people talk with their bodies as well as their mouths. When our body talks it is called **body language** or **non verbal communication**. Our body conveys messages to people by the way we dress, stand and sit. Our eyes convey messages, for example showing interest by being alert and looking at people or boredom by wandering and looking elsewhere.

What are the bodies saying in Fig 6.3? Choose from the list below (you may add your own ideas of what the bodies are saying too).

- Hurry up
- Do I have to wait all day
- I like you
- You are boring
- How interesting
- I like my job
- I hate my job

Fig 6.3 Body language

Remember that when you are face to face your body talks – so beware!

The spoken word

In both telephone communications and face to face communications the spoken word is important. For example we:

- welcome or greet callers
- ask the questions to find out their requirements, check our understanding and gain additional information
- hold a conversation
- answer questions and give information to the caller
- summarise information
- end the conversation.

Our tone of voice, its style and the vocabulary we use need to be appropriate.

Listening

When callers talk you need to listen and make appropriate noises and gestures to show you are understanding such as the occasional nod of your head, saying 'Yes' every now and then – but not too much or you can distract the caller and be irritating.

ACTIVITY

Read the conversation below and list the faults in the way James handled it.

Caller arrives at James' desk. James is busy sorting some papers for filing. The caller waits a few moments and then coughs to attract James' attention.

Caller   *Excuse me.*
James   *Afternoon. How can I help you? (James does not look up from his papers.)*
Caller   *I would like to speak to Mrs Hill please?*
James   *Do you 'ave an appointment? (Glancing up at the caller.)*
Caller   *No I don't. But I really do need to speak to her.*
James   *I'll just see if she is in. (James goes to see if Mrs Hill is in her office, leaving his papers on the desk. James returns.) I'm sorry she is not in. She has probably gone for lunch. Perhaps you could call back sometime this afternoon? (James continues sorting his papers.)*
Caller   *It's quite urgent. May I leave a message?*
James   *Yes, of course. (James puts his papers down, glances at his watch and searches for his message pad.)*
Caller   *My name is Mr Blake. I am a sales representative from Wilcocks Ltd. Perhaps Mrs Hill could give me a ring as soon as possible? It really is important that I speak to her.*
James   *OK. (James finds his pad and writes the message opposite. The caller leaves. James puts the pad into his drawer, puts his papers away and leaves the office to go for lunch.)*

TELEPHONE MESSAGE

Time: ~~1600~~ 1400   Date: 15th

Returning your call ☐

Mrs Hill —
Mr Bla~~ke~~ck called.
Can you phone him?

Will call again ☐

Please call back ☑

URGENT ☐

From: Janes
Telephone No:

R
Ryman

The written word

Letters

All businesses receive and send letters to people outside the firm. The firm may send out a wide range of letters, e.g:

- letters of enquiry
- letters of apology
- invitations
- letters giving information
- letters confirming arrangements or appointments
- letters of complaint
- letters of acceptance
- letters of appointment to successful job applicants
- letters of rejection to unsuccessful job applicants.

Wherever you work, therefore, you will need to be able to write letters like the ones above. Letters tell a story about the firm which is sending them. They can say 'we are a well organised firm', 'we have high standards' or they can give negative messages which can give the firm a bad image. You must remember that *letters speak*.

How do letters speak?

1 *The visual impact* – the design, layout and the overall appearance of the letter when it is received. Is it neat and clean or is it crumpled, thumbed and looks messy?

2 *The tone* – is the tone of the letter polite and friendly or abrupt and nasty? Vocabulary counts.

3 *The English* – are the spelling, punctuation and grammar correct or are there spelling errors and poor sentence structure?

What do letters say about the writer?

Letters tell a story about their writer. They can say:

- this person is friendly
- this person is arrogant
- this person is stupid
- this person is good at their job
- this person is angry.

Read the following letters and describe the sort of person who wrote each one.

1

Brown's Point of Sale Enquiry Ltd
Hey Street
GUILDFORD
Surrey GU2 1JN

15 September 1991

For the Attention of Mrs Pollock
Training Officer
W W Superstores Ltd
Golden Street
GUILDFORD
Surrey GU3 2AJ

Dear Mrs Pollock,

Further to your company having purchased LX 600 point of sale
equipment you are required to be available for a training session
given by our company on 21 September at 10.30 am. This is provided
under the contract of purchase at no cost to you.

Mr Lowe will arrive at your organisation at 10.15 promptly and has
been instructed to report to your reception. He will demonstrate
the equipment to you and give you basic instruction on the use of
the equipment.

Yours sincerely,

Mr A Marton, Training Department

2

Brown's Point of Sale Equipment Ltd
Hey Street
GUILDFORD
Surrey GU12 1JN

15 September 19--

For the Attention of Mr Bracewell
Training Officer
Jasons Ltd
GUILDFORD
Surrey GU6 4LT

Dear Mr Bracewell,

Your company has recently purchased LX 600 point of sale
equipment. I am aware that this equipment is new to you and that
because it is the latest model which has just arrived on the
market your staff will need substantial instruction on its use. I
would therefore like to take the opportunity to offer you some
instruction on the equipment and can provide you with a
demonstrator who will visit you at your place of work if this is
convenient for you.

I have arranged for Mr Lowe, who is our senior demonstrator, to
visit on 20 September at 10.30 am. I do hope this time is suitable
for you. If it is not please do not hesitate to let me know so that
I can arrange an alternative time.

If I do not hear from you I will ask Mr Lowe to report to your
reception arriving at 10.15 on 20th September.

Yours sincerely,

T Harper

T Harper (Ms)
Training Department

Business language

The letters which are sent from a business need to be business like. They need to use suitable language. An increasing number of firms have adopted a more relaxed and friendly tone and style than in the past, but often it comes down to who you are writing to and for what reason. If you are writing to someone who you have known for some time you are able to be more personal even though the letter is a business letter. If you do not know the person very well it is better to be more formal. There are some words and phrases which are *not* to be used at any time such as:

- at your earliest convenience . . .
- I am writing to tell you . . .
- this is a letter . . .
- as hereinbefore listed . . .
- with reference to your communication of the . . .

ACTIVITY   What could you write instead of the phrases above?

Structure and layout

Like an essay, a letter has a beginning, a middle and an ending. The beginning of the letter involves putting the letter into context in the opening paragraphs – 'Thank you for your letter . . .', 'With reference to . . .' – you could describe this paragraph as a scene setter. The middle comprises the main body of the letter – it is the message. The ending includes the actions required and/or a complimentary close such as:

- I look forward to hearing from you
- I hope you are able to attend the meeting
- If you have any problems with this please let me know
- If you would like further information please do not hesitate to contact me

A good business letter should be structured as follows:

- Addresses
- Date
- Salutation
- Opening paragraph
- Main paragraph
- Ending paragraph
- Complimentary close

Direct Computers Limited
Directors: P Thomas, V Thomas, Regd no: 109856 UK
24 Carlisle Boulevard, Bognor Regis BS4 2LN

Mr Canning
17 Brantree Avenue
Lincoln LN2 3MR

                                        12-9-19--

Dear Mr Canning

Thank you for your valuable order which we received
yesterday. It is receiving our immediate attention.

Unfortunately the printer that you specified is not
available at the moment and I would like to offer you the
LQ3450 model, which normally retails at £15 more than the
printer you ordered, for the same price. This is available
for immediate delivery. If this is acceptable please let me
know and I will send the system out for next day delivery.

Thank you once again for your order and please feel free to
contact us for any technical advice when the system
arrives. I am enclosing a copy of our catalogue of printer
ribbons, paper and disks which may be of interest to you
and can offer you 15 per cent discount on your first order
as an incentive to deal with us.

            Yours sincerely

            Patricia Thomas

            Patricia Thomas

There are accepted conventions about the layout of letters which make
them look good and business like, and which can be produced speedily.
Some examples of accepted letter layouts for business letters which are
word processed or typed are as follows:

1 **Fully blocked** – every line begins at the left-hand margin like the letter from Mr Marton.

2 **Blocked** – this is the same as fully blocked except that the date is shown on the right-hand side and the complimentary close is in a central position. The letter from Patricia Thomas uses this layout.

3 **Semi blocked** – this is the same as the blocked layout but each paragraph is indented and the complimentary close is a little to the right of centre.

Punctuation

Sometimes you will see that in business letters punctuation is omitted except for full stops at the end of sentences.

Other inclusions

Letters often include reference numbers, enclosures, subject headings and copies to.

Salutations and closes

The correct salutations and closes are as follows:

- Dear Sir   Yours faithfully
- Dear Madam   Yours faithfully

Note that 'faithfully' has a small 'f'.

- Dear Mr Canning   Yours sincerely
- Dear Mr Jones   Yours sincerely
- Dear Anoop   Yours sincerely

If you cannot remember which to use try remembering that 'Sir and sincerely, S and s is wrong.'

As mentioned above many firms tend to have a more relaxed and friendly tone than in the past and this is displayed in the following salutations and complimentary closes:

- Dear Pat   Kind regards
- Dear Tayaba   Yours

ACTIVITY

Look again at Mr Marton's letter right. There are a few changes to the letter to illustrate some of the points mentioned above. What do you notice? Make a list of the changes that you notice.

Brown's Point of Sale Equipment Ltd
Hey Street
GUILDFORD
Surrey GU12 1JN

Ref: MS/POS/T

15 September 19--

For the Attention of Mrs Pollock
Training Officer
W W Superstores Ltd
Golden Street
GUILDFORD
Surrey GU3 2AJ

Dear Mrs Pollock,

DEMONSTRATION AND TRAINING LX 600

Your company has recently purchased LX 600 point of sale
equipment. I am aware that this equipment is new to you and that
because it is the latest model which has just arrived on the
market your staff will need substantial instruction in its use. I
would therefore like to take the opportunity to offer you some
instruction on the equipment and can provide you with a
demonstrator who will visit you at your place of work if this is
convenient for you.

I have arranged for Mr Lowe, who is our senior demonstrator, to
visit on 21 September at 10.30 am. I do hope this time is suitable
for you. If it is not please do not hesitate to let me know so that
I can arrange an alternative time.

If I do not hear from you I will ask Mr Lowe to report to your
reception arriving at 10.15 on 21st September.

Yours sincerely,

A Marton, Training Department

enc.
copy to: Mr Lowe

Deadlines

When writing or preparing letters always ensure that you plan in advance. People often have to act on information contained in letters, e.g. Mrs Pollock in the letter above has to let Mr Marton know if the date and time for the demonstration are unsuitable. She has to keep her diary clear for the demonstration or reorganise events like meetings to enable her to attend. All of this takes time. Likewise it is no use receiving the letter after the date of the demonstration or by second class post on 21 September. Mr Lowe would have arrived unexpectedly to find that Mrs Pollock had a prior engagement and knew nothing about his visit.

Memos

If you wanted to write to someone who does not work in your organisation you would send a letter. If, however, you wanted to send a message to someone in your organisation for them to receive at work you would send a **memorandum** or **memo** for short. If you wanted to write to their home address you would send a letter.

Like the letter a memo should have a beginning, a middle and an ending. The beginning puts the message into context, the middle says what the message is and the ending gives or requests action or a complimentary close. It should be short and to the point, never long winded. There is no need to sign a memo since it has the sender identified already. Many organisations have their own layout for memos and some have memo pads where you would just need to fill in your message. Others do not and the style is therefore left to the sender. A basic memo, however, looks like the example given below.

MEMORANDUM

TO: Abigail Waring

FROM: Thomas Gabriel   DATE: 9-11---

SUBJECT: LOST FILE 'McBRIDE'

Last week I informed you that Mrs McBride's file was lost. I am pleased to report that this has now been found and I have written to Mrs McBride apologising for the delay in confirming the details she requested.
I am sorry for the inconvenience this has caused.

In the example memo you will notice that the message is short and simple and deals with only one point. Who the memo is from and who it is being sent to are identified and it is dated. The subject of the memo is identified too. Although some organisations have their own house style all memos contain this basic information. A reference number may also be shown so that the memo can be easily found after it has been filed away.

Summary

1 *Ensure that you are adequately prepared when making and receiving telephone calls.*

2 *Always be polite and courteous when speaking on the telephone because you represent the firm.*

3 *Take telephone messages with care and pass them on promptly.*

4 *Be cost-conscious when making telephone calls.*

5 *In face-to-face business, always acknowledge callers straight away, make them feel comfortable and do not keep them waiting.*

6 *Remember that your body conveys messages through body language.*

7 *Speak clearly when talking to callers.*

8 *Letters sent out of the firm should be well written and well presented.*

9 *A memo should be short and to the point.*

DATA PROCESSING AND INFORMATION PROCESSING

7

This unit aims to:

- *Describe what computer hardware and software is.*
- *Tell you the most common programmes used in business and briefly explain their purpose.*
- *Present some rules when producing, checking and correcting text.*
- *Explain the rules when using databases and spreadsheets.*

Data processing and information processing are concerned with information into and out of computers and are increasingly important in business.

Hardware and software

Computers can be found in all sorts of businesses for many different tasks. A computer is a tool of business – it is designed to make your life easier, to get more work done, and to let you do jobs that you could not do before – just like a calculator makes it easier to deal with figures or a van makes it easier to deliver loads of goods. We will be looking at what goes into a computer system, and what it can do?

Computers need both hardware and software to work. **Hardware** is the word for the actual machines – keyboards, printers, screens, scanners, processors – things that you can actually touch. **Software** is the word for the programmes and instructions that make the machine useful. If you do not have any software for a computer it will not function just as a lorry without a driver to direct it cannot deliver goods. Businesses use all kinds of different software, often called programmes to do different jobs. Some of the main types of programmes are listed below:

1 **Word processors** are programmes that allow you to type into the computer, save the work that you have typed in to the machine, call it back on to the screen, alter it if you want and print it. This can be a lot easier than using a typewriter if you have a lot of letters to compile which are very similar. Using a word processor you can alter names, addresses

Display screen

Disk drive and processor

Keyboard

Printer

Fig 7.1 A personal computer and a printer

and some of the details of the letter very quickly without having to retype the whole letter. Some other facilities that word processors offer include:

- **spelling checkers** tell you if a word is misspelled or mistyped

- **word counts and page counts** inform you how long a document is

- **blocking** allows you to move blocks of words around a document or to put parts of one document into another.

2 **Databases** are electronic filing programmes that let you store information on the computer rather than in paper files. In a database information can be sorted in many different ways very quickly. So, if you wanted a list of which of your 5000 customers are in Birmingham, you could get it in a matter of minutes, even if the files on the computer are filed in alphabetical order. The same task could take hours using a paper system. Another advantage of databases is that they do not take up a lot of space because you can get a large number of files onto a computer disk. Paper files could take up as much as 200 times the space.

3 **Spreadsheets** are sophisticated calculators. They are mainly used for working out accounts, adding up invoices and keeping track of money. The main advantages of spreadsheets are:

- they can take very complex calculations and do them very quickly;

- they let you 'try out' calculations so that you can find the best answer to a problem and

- they can draw graphs of figures for you.

4 **Desktop publishers** are programmes that let you put pictures and words together. They can normally help you to draw pictures, make headings, use different styles of writing in different sizes and lay out documents so that they look attractive. They are often used for producing advertising material, price lists, brochures and instructions.

5 **Integrated packages** allow you to do a combination of the tasks that each of the packages above will do. They are quite expensive and sometimes need special computers to run them. The advantage of an integrated package is that you can use parts of one programme in another. It is possible to use graphs from a spreadsheet in a word processed document, add a desktop published heading to a letter, include a table of your best customers from the spreadsheet into a report or take some figures from a database and put them into a spreadsheet.

There are many different versions of all the packages – like there are many different sports cars, executive cars and lorries – and they have special features and controls. Whatever system you are using it will have been chosen to help you to do your job more easily and you will be trained how to get the best out of it.

ACTIVITY

Ask at work, on your work experience placement or at college, what software they use and say whether it is a word processor, database, spreadsheet, desktop publisher or integrated package. For each one make a note of the name of the programme and any special features that it has. An example is included.

TYPE	NAME	FEATURE
Word processor	NewWord	Can print in italics Can work in columns

The actual machines that you use may vary a great deal. Some business computers cost a few hundred pounds, others cost tens of thousands. Naturally, the more you pay, the more you get and a very expensive system will probably be able to do more than a cheap one. This does not mean that a more expensive computer is automatically best for your business – you might be better with a cheaper machine that is easier to work as long as it will let you use all the software you need to get your work done.

Almost all computer systems have the same basic bits of hardware in them:

1 **Keyboards** allow you to type information into the computer. Some keyboards have a number pad like a calculator as well as the typewriter-like keyboard and they have some special keys that are not found on a typewriter. Whatever keyboard you use you will find that they are all fairly similar and if your one is any different you will be trained on how to use it.

2 **Monitor:** the computer screen is usually called a **visual display unit** or VDU for short. Many VDUs are one colour only – usually white, yellow or green letters and diagrams on a black background. Some others are able to show a full range of colours and can take pictures to as good a standard as a good TV or better in some cases. When you are using a VDU there are a few rules to follow:

■ Do not sit too close.
■ Find out if there is a maximum time that you are allowed to work on the machine without a break – and take breaks when you are allowed one.
■ Work in good light and adjust the brightness and contrast to make it as easy on your eyes as you can.

3 **Processor** The main part of the computer is called the processor, the part that takes the information in, works with it, and then sends it to the screen or to a printer. The processor will usually have a disk drive in it. **Disk drives** read information off the disk just like a CD player reads music off the disk. There are two types of disk that you will come across:

■ **Floppy disks** are ones that you can take out of the machine. They have to be protected from dust, strong light and excessive heat or cold if they are to work well.
■ **Hard disks** – inside the machine you can have a disk that will store information. These disks are fragile and must not be knocked or bumped. They can store a lot of information and transfer it onto the screen or printer very quickly.

4 **Printers** print words, pictures, graphs and diagrams from the computer onto paper. There are a few different types of printer and they all have advantages and disadvantages. Table 7.1 compares them.

TYPE	COST	QUALITY	RUNNING COST
Laser printer	High	Excellent	1–2p/sheet
Bubble jet	Medium	Very good	1–2p/sheet
Inkjet	Medium	Very good	1p+/sheet
24 pin matrix	Medium–low	Good/very good	Under 1p
Dot Matrix	Low–medium	OK/good	Under 1p

Table 7.1.
Types of
printer

Fig 7.2 A laser printer

ACTIVITY

Ask at work, on your work experience placement or at college which hardware they use. For each item make a note of the name of the machine, model and any special features that it has. An example is given.

TYPE	NAME	FEATURE
Printer (laser)	Hewlett Packard LaserJet	Can print to a very high quality Prints graphics very well Quiet so it does not get on your nerves

Producing text

One of the main uses for computers is to input text to a word processor. You may also have to use a typewriter in the office to produce documents and there are different types that you could find:

1 **Manual typewriters** are becoming quite rare in offices now – they are the old type of typewriter which operates by pushing a bar with a letter on it onto the paper with a ribbon in front of it to make the letter.

2 **Electric typewriters** are very similar to manual typewriters but they have a power supply so that you do not have to press the keys as hard.

3 **Electronic typewriters** are the most modern type of machine (*see* Fig 7.3). They will have either a golfball or a daisy wheel to make the letters on the paper. As they have a power supply they are easy to use and they often allow you to correct a few letters on the paper. Some have a small screen that shows a line of type before the typewriter prints it so that you can correct any errors before they appear on the page.

Fig 7.3   An electronic typewriter

Whatever machine you are using when you are inputting text and numbers to a computer or using a typewriter there is no substitute for practice. You will need to get a speed of 15 words per minute. This is not very fast and you should be able to reach this speed quite quickly. There are a few things that you need to remember:

- If you do have to correct something then make sure the correction is neat – that is easy on a word processor but liquid paper on a typewriter can be messy.
- Correct an error as soon as you see it – do not wait and go back later, you might forget.

- Treat anything you are asked to type as confidential – the person having it typed will trust you not to talk about it.
- If anything goes wrong with the machine that you are unable to fix, report it at once, giving as much detail as possible to help others pinpoint the fault.
- If you want to practise at college or at home to get better at inputting or typing try to use the sort of material to type that you would get at work.
- Try to get some practice with a few different types of material: letters, memos, reports, tables or whatever you have to type at work.

Checking and correcting

Businesses produce lots of paperwork that needs to be checked and corrected – a handwritten document might need instructions on it, a typed one might need checking for errors. When you are checking/correcting material there are a number of symbols and instructions to use which are shown in Fig 7.4.

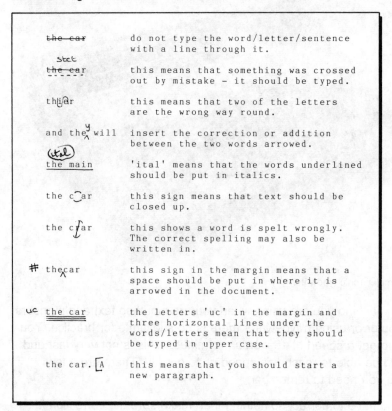

Fig 7.4 Correction symbols

These are the main correction signs that you will come across – there are a lot more that you will get to know if this is a large part of your job.

Type the letter shown in Fig 7.5, incorporating all the corrections that have been marked on it:

```
        15 September 19--


        Ms A Carter
uc      27 Broadacre lane
        LONDON      W9 3RU



        Dear Ms Carter

#       Thank you for the order for printer ribbons you sent
        us yesterday.  Unfortunately the ribbons that you
                                                    will be
        require are not in stock at the moment but we able
                                        weeks'
        to supply them in three days' time.


        I appreciate that this delay may be too long for you
          stet
        to wait and I will treat the order as cancelled
uc      unless i hear from you to the contrary in the next
NP      few days.  [I am very sorry that we are unable to
        supply you on this occasion and hope that you will
        not be put off from using our service in the future
        by this.


        Yours faithfully



                 s
        I Evan
uc      Director
```

Fig 7.5

Tips

- Make sure that you mark errors clearly – preferably use a good pencil or a pen in a different colour from the writing.
- Check numbers and calculations where you can – mark any errors so that someone else can correct them if you cannot.
- Make sure that the document is laid out in the way the company likes –

some firms have their own ways of doing things that you are supposed to use.

- If you are not sure what to do with a piece of text check with the writer and mark the text so a typist can tell what to do.
- Use double spacing to make it easier to correct errors.

Using computer databases and spreadsheets

Many firms keep information about the business on computers in a database – an electronic filing system. It is very important that the information that goes into a database is correct. Here are some rules to follow when putting information in:

- Make sure that you have the right record on screen before you change or update it (is this the right 'Smith, J' ?).
- When you enter data make sure that it is right before you press the return key to enter it (some programmes will ask you 'Is this correct Y/N?')
- If you are not sure about something – either the information that you have to put in, or how to use the system – *ask*.
- Do not gossip about the information that you have put into the computer. By asking you to do it they are trusting you to keep quiet about it.
- Make sure that the system is safe – are the plugs OK? Is it on a solid surface? Are there any cables which could trip people?
- Do not work on the system for too long – you will start to make mistakes and could get a headache. Ask how long you are allowed to work on the computer.
- Make backups of work that you have done as a matter of routine. If you do not you could lose all the information on a disk. If you do make backups you will only lose the work done since the last time you made a backup copy.
- If there is something wrong with the machine like a poor ribbon on the printer, fix it. If there is something wrong that you cannot fix report it, giving as much detail as you can to help repairs, e.g. 'The disk drive is making a whirring noise and I get a message saying "Disk Error reading Drive A" '.

You may also have to use a spreadsheet as part of your job, if you do, the rules above still apply to putting information into the spreadsheet. There are some special points that you need to keep in mind when using spreadsheets:

- It is very easy to make a mistake when you are inputting numbers – check carefully the information that you put in and, if you find that you are making a lot of errors, do something else for a few minutes to get your concentration back.
- Follow the instructions for the package carefully and look for any prompts or reminders on screen if you are not absolutely sure of what to do.
- If you are entering a formula or some other calculation make sure that it is right before you press the return key to enter it into the spreadsheet.

Use the letter below, which is about 150 words, and find the errors in it and mark them. When you have found and marked them, type the letter properly. Time yourself and, when you have finished, check that you do not have more than two errors like spelling mistakes, poor spacing or too much space between lines of text.

CARDWELL MACHINES LIMITED
17 HARDACRE GROVE
SALISBURY
WILTS.

Control limited
unit 3
Castle technology Park
Birmingham

28-09---

Your ref: crd/1098/h12t
Our ref: Jb-78104-rai

Dear Alan
Thankyou for your letter about the new product range. You certainly seem to have some good products and we'll be very interested to see some of them in action, particularly the updated 47 series controllers which Joan Carter, who has taken over from peter Haggerty, will be contacting you about. The main reason that I have contacted you is to ask you whether you've had any further thoughts about that proposal I made when I saw you last month? Your new range reminded me of it and I remembered that I'd said I'd call you about it — sorry I I forgot! Anyway, I've spoken to our technical people who think it will work but they'll need to work with some of your staff to put a test   machine together. If we go ahead Joan Carter will run our end of the project. I'm certainly keen and I think it'll make us some money. Let me know what you think.

Yours faithfully

J Khan
Managing Director

Keeping information secure

It is very important when you are using computers that you keep the information that you have on them safe. Because organisations have a lot of information about people on computers there is now a law, **the Data Protection Act (1984)**, which states that any firm that keeps details about people on computers has to register with the government. Once an organisation has registered they have to follow strict rules to make sure that the information they keep is:

- correct
- safe
- up to date.

This means that you have to be very careful about who you give information to from the computer. If someone calls in to the office for information and you do not know them you will need to check that they have permission. If you break these rules, both you and the organisation you work for could end up in court.

Summary

1 Computers need hardware and software to work – hardware describes the machines and software describes the programmes.

2 Some commonly used programmes are word processors, databases, spreadsheets, desktop publishers, and integrated packages.

3 There are two types of disks used – floppy disks and hard disks.

4 When word processing text, correct errors as soon as you see them.

5 A database is an electronic filing system.

6 Remember that data contained on a database is confidential.

7 Always make back-up copies of your files.

8 When using spreadsheets take care when inputting numbers.

9 Remember not to break the Data Protection Act.

PETTY CASH AND INVOICES

8

This unit aims to:

- *Explain what petty cash is.*
- *Tell you some basic rules for dealing with petty cash.*
- *Show you how to record petty cash transactions.*
- *Identify business documents used when buying and selling.*
- *Explain how to check invoices.*
- *Develop competencies in processing petty cash transactions and invoices.*

This unit deals with two basic types of financial transaction: petty cash and invoices.

Petty cash

Most organisations have **petty cash** – a fund that can be used to pay for small purchases. If someone has to go out and buy a single bottle of liquid paper because they have run out they can get the money from petty cash. When anyone has had to spend a small amount of money on something for the business they can keep the receipt and claim the money back from petty cash. Firms have petty cash for a number of reasons:

- If you have only a small purchase to make you may find it hard to persuade people to take a company order form.
- If someone has to pay for something out of their own pocket they can claim it back quickly.
- It can let you pay for small purchases, like window cleaning, easily.

In a small firm petty cash will only be a small amount of money – maybe £15 in a cashbox in someone's desk drawer which is topped up when it gets low. In a large firm it may be that they have a lot of petty cash transactions and spend a lot of money, possibly many thousands, each year. However much is involved there are a number of rules to follow:

Fig 8.1 A petty cash voucher

1 There will be a form to fill in to get petty cash, usually called a **petty cash voucher**. You normally have to have a receipt for the money that you have spent to attach to it and someone will have to sign to agree that you needed to spend the money.

2 Whenever you deal with cash there are some precautions to take:

- Never leave cash unlocked – always use a cash box, till, safe or some other secure place.
- Do not leave the box, drawer or whatever open. Make sure that the key is kept secure.
- Do not tell people where the money is, or how much there is unless they need to know.
- Avoid counting money near doors or windows if you can – you can be seen and someone could snatch the money from you.

3 Cash can be very dirty – always wash your hands before dealing with papers or eating food after handling money – you might save yourself an illness.

4 If there is anything that you cannot account for, or do not understand – ask. It is better to have something explained than to have the money short, or to fill in the transaction wrongly.

Keeping track of petty cash

The person who keeps petty cash records and issues petty cash payments is called the **petty cashier**. In some organisations the petty cashier is given a certain amount of money and makes a request for more when it is almost spent. Other organisations use what is called the **imprest** system. If this system is used a certain amount of money is allocated to petty cash, this is called the **imprest amount**. When the petty cashier works out how much has been paid out of petty cash in the week or month, then he/she is given this amount by the organisation's main cashier so that the imprest amount is restored. In this way the imprest acts a bit like a float in a till – as soon as some is used it is replaced.

As an example, Jonathan looks after the petty cash at Williamson's Ltd. The imprest amount is £50. Last week he paid £30 out of petty cash. The main cashier then gave him £30 when he produced the week's petty cash accounts to bring his total back up to the imprest amount of £50. At the end of this week he may only have used a few pounds and this is all that he will need from the main cashier to restore the imprest amount.

The petty cash book

Petty cash transactions can be recorded in a **petty cash book**.

PETTY CASH ACCOUNT								
Cash rec £	Date	Details	Voucher	Total paid £	Travel £	Postage £	Food £	Sundries £

Fig 8.2 An example of a page from a petty cash account book

You will notice in the example that there is a column for cash received. An amount of money will be entered in that column when the cashier gives the petty cashier money. There is also a cash paid column (total paid). When the petty cashier gives an employee petty cash the amount paid out is entered in this column. The columns on the right of the total paid column are called analysis columns. The number of analysis columns depends on what the firm finds useful. The analysis columns are there so that the firm can see at a glance the breakdown of petty cash expenditure. The main areas of expenditure can each have an analysis column so there may be a column for meals or stationery for example. The sundries (or miscellaneous) column is for recording any item of expenditure which does not have a separate analysis column. When each of the analysis columns is totalled and the totals are added together the figure obtained should equal the total of the total paid column.

Completing the petty cash book

Study the way in which the petty cash book is completed in the example below.

Jonathan, who works at Williamson's Ltd, is entering transactions into the petty cash book. He started the week with the imprest amount of £50. His transactions for the week beginning Monday 5 November are as follows:

Monday
Paid postage £5.00 on voucher no. 32.
Paid travel 75p on voucher no. 33.

Tuesday
Paid £4.50 on voucher no. 34, £4.00 for a plant for the office and 50p for biscuits.

Wednesday
Paid £3.00 for taxi fare on voucher no. 35.
Paid £2.00 for window cleaning on voucher no. 36.

Thursday
Paid £4.00 for lunch and £1.50 for travel expenses on voucher no. 37.

Friday
Paid £5.56 for cleaning materials on voucher no. 38.
Received cash necessary to restore the imprest.

Dr								Cr
PETTY CASH ACCOUNT								
Cash rec £	Date	Details	Voucher	Total paid £	Travel £	Postage £	Food £	Sundries £
50 · 00	5 Nov	Balance b/d						
	5 Nov	Postage	32	5 · 00		5 · 00		
	5 Nov	Travel	33	0 · 75	0 · 75			
	6 Nov	Plant / biscuits	34	4 · 50			0 · 50	4 · 00
	7 Nov	Travel	35	3 · 00	3 · 00			
	7 Nov	Sundries	36	2 · 00				2 · 00
	8 Nov	Food/Trav	37	5 · 50	1 · 50		4 · 00	
	9 Nov	Sundries	38	5 · 56				5 · 56
				26 · 31	5 · 25	5 · 00	4 · 50	11 · 56
26 · 31	9 Nov	Cash Received						
	9 Nov	Balance c/d		50 · 00				
76 · 31				76 · 31				
50 · 00	10 Nov	Balance b/d						

Fig 8.3

This is how to complete the petty cash book.

1 The imprest amount is £50. This is entered into the cash received column on the left hand side. The data is entered and the details completed by writing 'Balance b/d', which means 'balance brought down'. This is the amount of money in the cashbox at the start of the week.

2 On Monday Jonathan paid two lots of petty cash, £5 for postage voucher no. 32 and 75p for travel on voucher no. 33. Each voucher is dealt with in turn. Enter appropriate date, in the details column write 'postage', write 32 in the voucher column, £5 in the total paid column and £5 in the postage column. On the next line write in the date again, the details (travel), the voucher (33), the total payment (75p) and write 75p in the travel column.

3 On Tuesday Jonathan paid £4.50 on voucher no. 34, £4.00 was paid for a plant for the office and 50p for biscuits. The transaction is recorded by writing in the date, details (plant/biscuits), the voucher (34), the total payment (£4.50) and then write £4.00 in the sundries column (because there is not a special analysis column for plants) and 50p in the food column.

4 Continue entering the other transactions until all the transactions have been entered.

5 When all the entries have been made, draw a line under the total paid and analysis columns and total each of these columns. Then underline the totals in the analysis columns twice but do not underline the total of the total paid column.

6 Add up all the totals of the analysis columns and check that it equals the total of the total paid column. If it does not, check your additions and your entries are correct because you have made an error.

7 The cashier will give you an amount equal to the total amount which has been paid out to restore the imprest. In this case it is £26.31. This figure is written into the cash received column, the date is entered and 'cash received' is written into the details column.

8 The petty cash book is now to be balanced. Follow this part carefully as some people find it a bit tricky. There are now two amounts in the cash received column (£50 and £26.31), add these together making £76.31, and write this figure into the cash received column, draw a line above it and underline it twice. On the same line of the petty cash book write this figure into the total paid column, draw a line above it and underline it twice.

9 You now need to insert an amount of £50 into the line above these totals in the total paid column as a balance in order to make the amounts in the total paid column add up to £76.31. Then enter the date, and in the details column enter 'Balance c/d'. This means balance carried down.

10 Finally, the balance is 'brought down' to start the new week. In the cash received enter £50 (the imprest amount has been restored), the date is 10 Nov, and the details is 'Balance b/d'.

ACTIVITY

Jonathan is off sick and you have been asked to keep the petty cash book up to date until he returns. Write up the next week's transactions and balance the petty cash book (copy Fig 8.4 onto a clean sheet of paper). These are the transactions:

Monday
Paid travel £2.50 on voucher no. 39.
Paid for stamps £2.00 on voucher no. 40.

Wednesday
Paid £15.96 for lunches on voucher no. 41.
Paid £2.00 for window cleaning on voucher no. 42.

Thursday
Paid £2.50, £1.00 for dusters and £1.50 for furniture polish on voucher no. 43.

Friday
Received cash necessary to restore the imprest.

PETTY CASH ACCOUNT								
Cash rec £	Date	Details	Voucher	Total paid £	Travel £	Postage £	Food £	Sundries £
50.00	12 Nov	Balance b/d						

Fig 8.4

Invoices

This section deals primarily with processing invoices (bills), which is one of the clerical tasks you need to be competent in. This section, however, also briefly covers some other business documents which you will encounter at work.

When a firm wants to buy something from another firm it normally completes a special order form, called a **purchase order**, to tell the supplier what it wants to buy. When the seller delivers the goods requested a **delivery note** is given to the buyer. This delivery note details what is actually being delivered, which may not be the same as what has been ordered, e.g. the seller may not have had a particular product in stock.

In a large organisation there will be a stores department where deliveries will be received and the delivery note checked against the actual delivery. This is to ensure the delivery is correct and that the goods are in a satisfactory order. In a small organisation the owner/manager may do this or another member of staff. The delivery note is then signed by the buyer and is given to the person delivering the goods – a copy is retained by the buyer for reference. In some firms the buyer completes a **goods received note** to itemise what has actually been received.

So far goods have been ordered and received but payment has yet to be made. The seller now sends the buyer an **invoice** which is a bill for the goods delivered. The invoice is checked and corrected if necessary and payment is made to the seller. If some of the goods are later returned to the selling firm a **credit note** is issued by the selling firm to the buyer to say that a certain sum of money is owing to the buyer. If for any reason the invoice which the seller sent was less than it should have been and this smaller amount was paid by the buyer then the seller will send the buyer a **debit note** to tell the buyer how much is still outstanding. Sometimes the two firms buy and sell to each other on a regular basis, in which case the seller sends the buyer a **statement of account** at the end of each month showing the cost of goods purchased, the amount paid to date and the amount still owing.

Re-read the above paragraph explaining about the flow of documents between the buyer and seller and complete the flow chart below. In this example assume that the name of the buying firm is 'Brownings Ltd' and the name of the selling firm is 'Jackson & Sons Ltd'.

ACTIVITY

> Brownings Ltd wishes to buy some products from
>
> Jackson & Sons Ltd. Browning Ltd completes an
>
> . . . .
>
> and sends it to Jacksons & Sons Ltd.

↓

Jackson & Sons Ltd send the delivery to Brownings Ltd.
The van driver who is delivering the goods gives a

....

to the staff who are receiving the delivery at
Brownings Ltd. The goods are checked against the

....

↓

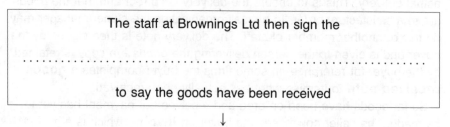

The staff at Brownings Ltd then sign the

....

to say the goods have been received

↓

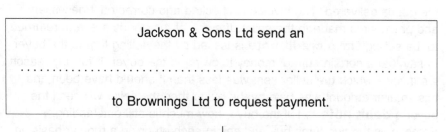

Jackson & Sons Ltd send an

....

to Brownings Ltd to request payment.

↓

Brownings Ltd checks that everything is in order and
sends a cheque to Jackson & Sons to pay for the goods.

Processing invoices

An invoice is a bill sent between businesses requiring payment for goods
or services (*see* Fig 8.6). It may, for example, be for supplying the firm
with goods or repairing a photocopier. Whatever the invoice is for, it needs
to be paid. What you will be learning here is how to process an invoice for
payment, or making sure that it is correct for the organisation to pay it.
Before you pay an invoice you need to check that the goods or service
received were satisfactory. In most cases this is quite easy as there will
be a copy of the delivery note on file itemising the goods received, which
will have been signed by whoever checks the job on completion or goods
on delivery.

To process an invoice for payment you need to:

PART B: BUSINESS SUPPORT SYSTEMS

1 Check that the service provided was to a satisfactory standard or that the goods have been received and were in good condition. This will normally mean checking that there is a delivery note on file and that it has been signed to show the job or goods are acceptable. The invoice may have been initialled by a person in the firm who is authorised to say that the invoice is to be paid.

2 A buyer may request a **quotation** from the seller. This lets the buyer know the price of the goods before ordering them. If a quotation has been requested, check that the price of the goods on the invoice is the same as on the quotation. The seller cannot change the price for that order unless the buyer has agreed to this.

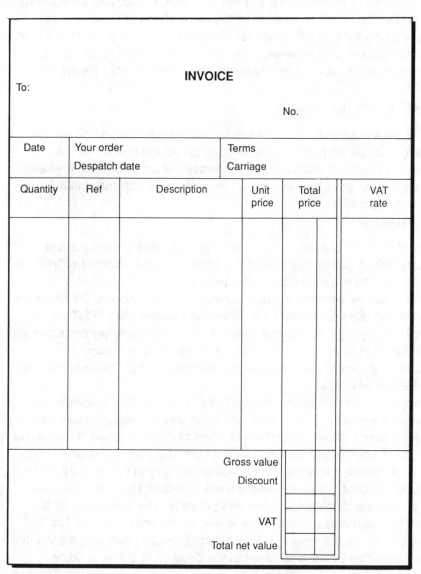

Fig 8.5 A typical invoice

3 Check that the calculations are correct on the invoice and that you have not been overcharged for anything.

Once you have checked the invoice you can pass it on for payment. In order to do this you would normally use a rubber stamp on the invoice which will indicate that everything is in order.

If there are any differences between what the invoice charges and what you received, if prices have altered or there is an error in the calculations, you will need to mark this on the invoice and pass it on to whoever deals with these. You may simply attach a note to the invoice but many firms have special cards to let you know what is wrong with the invoice. If you were required to deal with this yourself you could contact the selling firm and explain the problem, or arrange to send a cheque for the correct amount and a letter to the seller detailing the error or simply a copy of the corrected invoice. Organisations have their own procedures for how to deal with such problems and whatever they are you should always follow them.

Checking the figurework

On the invoice example you can see the figures everywhere. When passing invoices for payment you need to be able to check that the figurework is correct. Mistakes are made even when computers are used to generate the invoices because the computer operator may input incorrect information.

You need to:

1 Check that the quantity received and the unit price are correct and multiply them together to give you the amount without discount or VAT (in the example 10 chairs at £50 each equals £500)
2 Check that the percentage trade discount is correct and that the total trade discount has been calculated correctly (in the example 5% of £500 equals £25). Trade discount is a special discount given to firms simply because they are in business or are 'trade' normally because they buy in bulk.
3 Subtract the trade discount from the initial amount (in the example £500 less £25 equals £475).
4 Now you need to calculate the VAT. Value Added Tax is charged on most business sales and is calculated when *all* the discounts have been deducted from the total regardless of when payment is made. To calculate the VAT, therefore, you deduct both the trade discount and cash discount. You have already deducted the trade discount so you now need to deduct the cash discount. The cash discount is a reduction for prompt payment and encourages firms to pay their bills promptly. The cash discount is stated as a percentage. If you look at the invoice above you will find it above the 'Price' columns. It states 'Terms 2.5% 28 days' and means that if you pay within 28 days you will have a discount of 2.5%. In some invoices the cash discount is printed on the bottom of the invoice. To calculate the cash discount you multiply the amount excluding VAT by the

```
                    JACKSON & SONS LTD
                    Parkway Industrial Estate
                    Sutton, Surrey S98 5PR

                          INVOICE

To: Brownings Ltd
    82/84 High Street
    RICHMOND   TW9 8RD                    No. 0189467
```

Date	Your order 7690	Terms 2.5% 28 days
12/12/--	Despatch date 4/12/--	Carriage

Quantity	Ref	Description	Unit price	Total price		VAT rate
10		Office chairs	£50	£500	00	
		Less trade discount at 5%		£25	00	
			Gross value	£500	00	
			Discount	£ 25	00	
				£475	00	
			VAT	81	05	
			Total net value	£556	05	

Fig 8.6

the percentage cash discount. In the example given it is £475.00 multiplied by 2.5% which gives £11.87.

The amount obtained after deducting all discounts is £463.13 (obtained by subtracting trade discount of £25.00 from £500.00 leaving £475.00, and then subtracting cash discount of £11.87 from £475.00). This net figure is not shown on the invoice but is calculated so that the VAT can be determined. Now you calculate the VAT on this net amount of £463.13 by multiplying this figure by 17.5%. This gives £81.05 VAT.

5 Finally, add the VAT to the amount excluding VAT to obtain the total amount due. (In the above example £475.00 add £81.05 equals £556.05)

6 If your firm does not pay the invoice within the period stated the discount for prompt payment is lost and you would pay the amount shown on the invoice. If your firm pays within the period enabling the cash discount to be received then the cash discount is deducted from the Amount Excluding VAT and then the VAT as shown on the invoice is added. In the example shown in Fig 8.6, you would calculate 2.5% of £475.00, giving £11.87 and subtract it from £475.00, giving £463.13, and then add the VAT which is £81.05 which gives £544.18 as the amount due.

Check the invoice shown in Fig 8.7. The goods have been received and are in good order. Would you pass the invoice for payment? If not explain why not?

JACKSON & SONS LTD
Parkway Industrial Estate
Sutton, Surrey S98 5PR

INVOICE

To: Brownings Ltd
    82/84 High Street
    RICHMOND   TW9 8RD   No. 763986

Date 18 Jan 19--	Your order 7690 Despatch date 11/1/19--	Terms 2.5% 28 days Carriage

Quantity	Ref	Description	Unit price	Total price		VAT rate
10		Office desks Less trade disc at 5%	£150	£1500 250	00 00	

			Gross value	4750	00	
			Discount			
			VAT	712	50	
			Total net value	£4037	50	

Fig 8.7

Summary

1 *Petty cash is a fund to pay for small purchases.*

2 *A petty cash voucher is completed when someone wants petty cash.*

3 *Petty cash transactions are recorded in a petty cash book.*

4 *The following business documents are used when goods are bought and sold. Purchase Order; Delivery Note; Goods Received Note; Invoice; Debit Note; Credit Note; Statement of Account.*

5 *Before you pay an invoice you should check that:*
- *Goods or services were received and were satisfactory*
- *The prices shown on the invoices are correct*
- *The calculations on the invoice are correct.*

STOCK HANDLING

This unit aims to:

- *Identify the type of stock kept in an office.*
- *Explain the reasons for keeping track of stock.*
- *Show you how to keep track of stock.*
- *Develop competency in stock handling.*

This unit is about keeping track of the stock in an office, issuing it correctly when it is needed and keeping the records up to date.

In most firms there are some stocks kept in the office of items such as biros, paperclips, staplers, liquid paper and typewriter ribbons. This stock is quite expensive and, in some cases, like liquid paper thinners, can be dangerous if not properly stored. It needs to be kept:

- **safe** – to avoid accidents;
- **secure** – to avoid theft; and
- **stocked up** – to avoid running out.

There are a number of stages in keeping track of stock:

- Checking that deliveries match orders and letting your supervisor know if there are errors.
- Storing stock safely and securely and updating the **stock record cards** to show how much stock there is (*see* Fig 9.1).
- Checking the stock to make sure that you actually have in stock what the books say you should have – a **stock check** – and reporting any errors as soon as possible.
- Providing people with the stock they need from a **requisition** quickly, safely and in the right amounts and then updating your records to show what stock you have left.
- Reordering, or asking for goods to be reordered, when you get low on them. There is normally a **reorder level** and **reorder quantity** so that you know how much to order and when.
- Making sure that all the records of **stock movements** are neat, clear and up to date.

When dealing with stock there are a few useful tips:

- Get to know the forms for ordering, recording and reordering stock so that you can find what you want to know.

STOCK RECORD CARD

| ITEM: | | REORDER LEVEL: | |
| SUPPLIER: | | REORDER QUANTITY: | |

Date	Received	Issued	Balance

Fig 9.1 A stock record card

STOCK REQUISITION   No

| From: | | Date: |

Qty	Ref	Description

Authorisation:

Fig 9.2 A stock requisition card

- Keep records up to date. Do not leave items to enter later in case you forget.
- Make sure that the stock is kept tidy. It will then be easier to keep track of, less likely to be damaged and you will be able to find things faster.
- Get people to ask you for things before they run out by going round and checking their supplies so that they will not have to come to you in a hurry.
- If you have any inflammable materials to store make sure that there is a fire extinguisher handy.

- Check the area where you store stock for hazards and security risks and report any you find.
- Store the most commonly required items where you can get at them easily.
- Follow the storage instructions on packets – if something says 'Do not stack more than three high' then *do not*.
- Make estimates rather than counting items that would be hard to count and are not expensive, like paperclips or rubber bands.
- Find out how to put an emergency order through if there is a rush.
- Find out what the rules are for petty cash, in case you have to go and buy something.

ACTIVITY

The stock record card illustrated here for an item in a stationery store is wrong. Look at the stock card and identify any errors.

STOCK RECORD CARD

ITEM: Liquid Paper   REORDER LEVEL: 10

SUPPLIER: Office Supplies Ltd   REORDER QUANTITY: 30

Date	Received	Issued	Balance
8 January			15
9 January		5	10
9 January		2	8
10 January		1	7
15 January		1	6
16 January	30		35
17 January		3	31
18 January		1	29

Fig 9.3

Summary

1 *Stock control in offices is necessary to keep office stock safe and secure, and to avoid running out of materials and equipment needed.*

2 *Learn about the stock control system used in your office.*

3 *Always keep stock records up-to-date.*

4 *Follow storage instructions and follow safety rules when dealing with inflammable materials.*

MAIL HANDLING

This unit aims to:

- *Distinguish between internal and external post.*
- *Give reasons for dealing with mail efficiently and carefully.*
- *Outline procedures for dealing with incoming and outgoing mail.*
- *Identify postal services.*

This unit is about being able to handle post and mail which every organisation has to deal with.

There are two sets of post/mail – internal and external:

- **Internal post** is mail sent by one person in the organisation to another person in the same organisation. This could be within a building or, if you work for a large organisation, at another site.
- **External post** is mail sent outside the firm or received from outside the organisation. This will normally be sent by ordinary post but there are also other methods of sending goods and letters including rail, carrier services, couriers, fax and telemessages.

It is important for mail to be dealt with efficiently and carefully for a number of reasons:

- There may be money/valuables in the post.
- Orders and enquiries have to be answered as soon as possible.
- The organisation cannot answer queries that are lost in the post.
- There may be a security risk in some organisations, for example some shops have had letter bombs delivered to them because they sell fur coats.
- It may be necesary to indicate when post was received, e.g. when a bill was paid, or when a letter was received.

In a small organisation the owner or manager may deal with receiving and opening the mail and sending out post. Many small firms have little, if any, internal mail because the staff tend to see each other frequently and are not separated by distance (e.g. different buildings, different offices), although it is not unusual for members of staff to leave notes and messages for each other.

In a large organisation, however, there is normally a special room, called the **mail room** or **post room**, with special staff set aside to deal with all the internal and external mail. Departments within organisations normally have a member of staff from the department distributing the mail when it is delivered to the department. Regardless of how the mail is distributed or prepared for **despatch** (i.e. for sending out of the firm) there are certain basic rules and if mail handling does not go smoothly serious problems can arise as the following activity shows.

ACTIVITY

Read the tales told by supervisors and managers about what went wrong in the organisation due to poor mail handling. Then read the *rules for handling mail* below and identify which rule(s) were broken in each case.

The sales manager's tale: We had been dealing with a customer who wanted a large order but needed it delivering immediately. The rules are such that we need to have large orders in writing. One week later we had an irate customer on the phone claiming that we did not meet the delivery date promised. When we explained that we had not received the order in writing and therefore could not despatch the goods the customer was furious and said that the order was posted first class on the morning of the day the enquiry was made. The customer found another supplier and we have never had any business since. Two weeks later the order form turned up in the office – it had been passed to another employee with the same surname as mine but she worked in marketing and not in sales.

The accounts supervisor's tale: According to our records a customer had not paid his account. We sent the customer a final demand and still did not receive payment. We sent another letter threatening court action if payment was not made and finally we put the matter in the hands of the solicitor. The customer wrote to the company at a later date, obviously very angry and threatening all sort of actions. The customer claimed to have sent payment before going on holiday. On returning from holiday the customer found a letter notifying him of court action for non-payment. We were really very embarrassed when the cleaner found the envelope containing payment of the bill between two desks.

The public relations officer's tale: I received a complaint from a furious client who was not very complimentary about our firm. I wrote a letter of apology, a real grovelling letter. I wrote first class on the envelope because I thought it better to send a reply as quickly as possible. Imagine my horror when the client sent me another even more insulting letter billing me for the postage she had to pay on the letter I sent her. It had been posted without a stamp! I don't think I'll ever forget, especially since I was in charge of public relations.

The account manager's tale: I had a customer who claimed to have sent payment for an invoice before the due date so that the discount for prompt payment could be claimed. The debtor's section which was responsible for receiving payment claimed to have received the payment after the due date. The customer claimed to have sent payment well before the due date and said that he could not be held responsible for our inefficiency. Unfortunately, the date received had not been stamped on the correspondence and so we had no proof on when we actually received payment. This customer was a good customer but relations have never been the same since then.

State which of the rules were broken in each of the four employees' accounts.

These four horror stories are typical of what can happen when things go wrong. Handling mail correctly requires following certain procedures and rules. Some rules worth following are given below, though most businesses will have their own additional rules.

Rules for handling mail

Incoming mail

1 Ensure that you have a good, clear, clean space to work at.
2 Open the envelopes unless they are marked private or confidential.
3 Take out the contents of envelopes dealing with each envelope in turn:

- Date-stamp the contents of the envelope.
- Staple enclosures to the letters.
- Enclosures are normally indicated by 'Enc' at the bottom left of the letter. Sometimes the actual enclosures are listed too.
- If an enclosure is missing make a note of it.

- If the envelope contains money in any form, e.g. a cheque, postal order or cash, it should be recorded in the **remittances book**.
- If there are valuable documents in the envelope do not staple them directly to the letter – put them into an envelope, label the contents clearly with the contents such as 'Driving Licence' and staple the envelope to the letter making sure you miss the document inside.

4 Re-check the envelope to ensure that it is empty.
5 Take care throughout not to drop any envelopes or enclosures.
6 Once all the mail has been opened and dealt with as explained above sort the mail into batches so that it is easy to distribute. You may sort the mail in a convenient way, e.g. by department or by person. It helps if you know who is who in the organisation and what the departments are responsible for.

Internal mail

Internal mail is collected and redistributed in a similar way.

Outgoing mail

1 The letters will normally go by second class unless they are marked otherwise. Letters are weighed if they look too bulky or seem too heavy for the minimum first or second class post or they are going abroad.
2 They are franked or stamped as appropriate.
3 Recorded deliveries and registered mail will need to be taken to the post office.
4 Make sure that all this is completed in time for the post office to pick up the mail or for you to take it to the post office if they do not collect directly from you.

Even if you do not work in the mail room but deal with the mail in your office or section the procedures are just the same. In many firms the mail is distributed to departments, sections or particular people unopened and so receiving the mail in the way described above is still necessary. Organisations may have additional rules that need to be followed, e.g. supervisors may need to sign that enclosures are missing or payment has been received.

Putting letters and enclosures in envelopes

Most jobs require letters and/or documents to be put into envelopes and the envelopes sealed ready for sending out of the firm. Read how a polytechnic student on work experience approached the task of putting bills into envelopes.

A BTEC First student was on work experience and was working in the accounts department of a large firm along with a student from the polytechnic. The student from the polytechnic was asked to put some bills into envelopes. The envelopes had the name of the recipient typed on them. The BTEC First student watched in amazement and this is what he saw.

The polytechnic student put the bills into the envelopes one after the other daydreaming. He sealed each envelope once he had inserted the bill. He then realised that he had made an error and tried to find the fault – of course he could not because he had sealed the envelopes. So he opened all the envelopes and threw them away, took some window envelopes out of his drawer and put the folded bills into those. He piled them up one on top of the other. When they reached a certain height they toppled over because they could not balance any more. While he was picking them up he noticed that he had put the bills into the envelopes back to front so that the address did not show at all . . .

This story is so ridiculous it must be true. The polytechnic student had not learnt some basic rules because he had never had to deal with such a large volume of mail. He had over 100 bills to despatch. When you have to deal with outgoing mail like this you should:

1 Staple enclosures to the letter.
2 Check the name and address on the letter if it has been typed on and check the name and address on the correspondence.
3 Put the correspondence into the correct envelope leaving the envelope unsealed.
4 When all the correspondence has been correctly put into the envelopes seal the envelopes.

A final word on safety

When dealing with mail there is often equipment involved. Take care to use it safely and in the manner in which you have been trained. Do not use equipment unless you have been trained to do so. There are a number of pieces of equipment that you will come across in a mail room:

1 **Postal scales** – sensitive scales that let you enter the postal rates and, when you weigh a package, will tell you how many stamps it needs or how much to frank it. They will normally only weigh items up to a few kilograms (*see* Fig 10.1).
2 **Letter opening machines** allow you to feed envelopes into the machine which then slits them open at the very top. This can be a lot faster than opening letters by hand but care has to be taken with these machines as they have sharp blades to open the letters and can jam if an item that is too thick is put through.

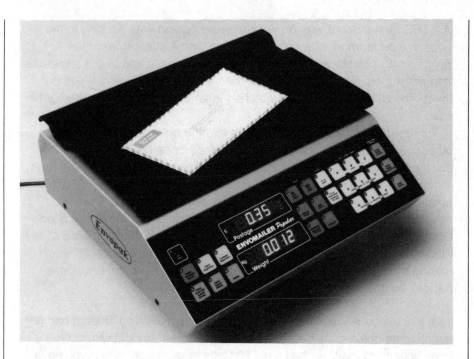

Fig 10.1 A postal weighing machine

3 **Franking machines** – rather than putting a stamp on a letter a franking machine prints a stamp known as a frank on the letter and this serves the purpose of a stamp. Firms use franking machines because letters can be put through them quickly and they can often put some form of message or advert onto the frank. The franking machine is 'loaded' with a certain amount of money and the operator then puts letters through until there is no credit left. There are all sorts of different models (some very sophisticated ones will weigh a letter, seal it, automatically put the right value frank on it and pass it on for posting; simpler machines have to be set by hand and operate more slowly).

4 **Letter sealers** will seal letters that are fed into them. Some of the more sophisticated ones will also fold pages and put them into envelopes before sealing them.

Sending post

There are a number of ways of sending letters and parcels – the list below shows some of the main 'carriers', the sort of items they will deal with, the service they offer and an idea of the cost.

CARRIER/SERVICE	ITEMS CARRIED AND SERVICE	COST
Post Office		
1st class mail	Letters and parcels Usually next day delivery for letters, longer for parcels	Low
2nd class mail	Letters and parcels Two to three days for letters, can be a week for parcels	Low
Recorded delivery	Letters and parcels Used for valuable items if you need proof that they have been delivered	More than mail
Registered post	Letters and small parcels Used for valuable items if you need proof of delivery and some compensation if they are lost or damaged	More than mail
Swiftair	Letters and small parcels Used for sending urgent items abroad and provides a quick service	Medium
Datapost	Letters and medium parcels Guarantees that the item will be delivered on the next working day in this country and is very quick to addresses abroad	High
British Rail Red Star	Letters and parcels Next day delivery for urgent items which can be collected from you	High
British Rail	Parcels Delivery of parcels and proof of delivery to most parts of the country	Low
Private carriers	Letters and parcels There are a lot of private carriers who will take letters and parcels for you. The services they offer and the cost need to be checked with them. Check them out in the *Yellow Pages* under 'Courier Services'	Med–high

For each of the letters listed below say what service you would use to send them out of the organisation. An example is given.

ITEM	SEND BY:
A mailshot of 500 letters trying to sell some of your products	2nd class mail
A contract for £25 000 that you must get to the firm the next day	
A letter to an employee asking if they would like to join the staff club	
A parcel to go to a firm in France as soon as possible	
£300 in cash to be sent as quickly as possible to a sales rep who has had his wallet stolen while staying at a hotel	

Summary

1 *An organisation deals with two types of mail, internal and external.*

2 *Mail needs to be dealt with quickly and efficiently.*

3 *Large organisations have a mail room and specialist staff to deal with the mail.*

4 *Many firms have set rules for handling mail which must be followed at all times to avoid problems arising.*

5 *Be careful with equipment used when dealing with mail and only use equipment which you have been trained to use and are authorised to use.*

6 *There are various postal services. Use the most appropriate service and be aware of costs.*

REPROGRAPHICS

This unit aims to:

- *Explain various ways of copying documents.*
- *Give you practical tips to follow when making copies and passing on copies.*
- *Help you to be cost conscious when making copies.*

Reprographics is about making copies of documents. In the office there are a number of ways you can do this:

1 Photocopier – probably the best known way to copy documents. The photocopier is quick, quiet and easy to use and can have all sorts of facilities for reducing or enlarging, collating and colour copying. It is quite expensive per copy for a long run and, if it goes wrong, it can be costly and time consuming to fix. Photocopiers need to be filled up with toner, and this can be quite expensive.

2 Spirit copier – not very often used in the office. To use a spirit copier you have to type onto a special sheet and put this onto the spirit copier. It tends to produce pale copies and the quality is not good, but it is easy to use, cheap to run and simple to prepare. The spirit which is used is highly inflammable and can be dangerous if not stored properly.

3 Offset litho – used for long runs of copies as they are messy to use, difficult to set up and noisy. An offset lithograph needs a special master copy to be made and this is then put onto the machine for printing. It produces good results and can print in more than one colour though changing from one colour to another takes a long time and a lot of work.

You will almost certainly use a photocopier for most of your copying at work. Photocopiers vary from small simple machines to very big machines with numerous features and you will probably need some help to use yours at first.

Here are some tips to remember when making copies:

- Make sure that you have the original on the copier in the right place.
- Check that the copier controls are set to do what you want – do not hit the print button and then realise the person before you has left the machine set for twenty A3 copies when you want three A4 copies.
- Try to sort documents into sets as they are copied rather than taking a whole lot of paper and then trying to sort it.

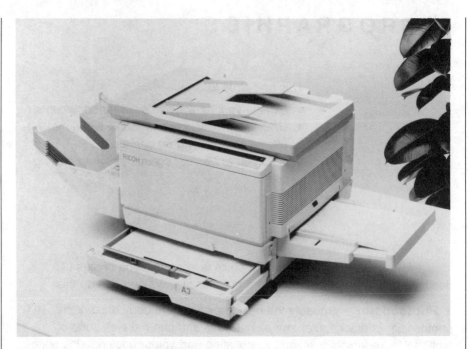

Fig 11.1 A photocopying machine

- If the machine does not work check for obvious faults. Is there paper in it? Is the toner low? Are there any lights on it to indicate faults? Is there a troubleshooting guide? If you cannot see what is wrong or cannot fix it then report the fault promptly with as much detail as you can.
- Sort your papers out before you go on to the copier so you do not hold people up leafing through a file looking for the page to copy.
- Use the contrast/darkness control to make sure that copies are clear.
- Keep both originals and copies clean and neat – a folder is a good way of making sure that they do not get crumpled or dirty.
- If you are the last person to use the machine for the day, switch it to standby (*do not* unplug it unless you have been told to – some machines need to be left plugged in) when you have finished.
- If you are enlarging or reducing a page, try a single copy to make sure you have the machine set correctly before running off a lot of copies.
- If you have to enter copies into a book or record them some other way make sure that you do this – it is often used to make sure that the machine is regularly serviced and to charge users for copying.

Here are some tips to remember when passing copies on:

- Fasten multipage sets together securely having made sure that the pages are in the right order.
- If you have to send copies by internal post or outside the company make sure that they are clearly addressed.

- If something is urgent use first class post (or whatever other service your firm uses such as a courier) or, for internal mail, mark it 'Urgent'.
- If the material is confidential make sure that it is sealed securely in an envelope and that it is marked 'Private', 'Personal', 'Confidential', 'For the attention of . . .' or some other wording.
- Do not discuss confidential material you have copied – by asking you to do the copying you are trusted not to gossip about it.
- Pass originals back to the person who asked for the copying indicating that the work has been done.
- If there is some reason why work cannot be done in a reasonable time tell the person why, politely. Do not just leave it. It could be important and, if so, it will have to be copied elsewhere.
- See if the machine has any special features that could make it easier to do lots of copies or to copy multi page documents, like an automatic sheet feeder or a collator. If it has, ask to be shown how to use them.
- Check that the quality of a copy is acceptable before you send it out. This is especially important if you are sending documents out of the organisation as poor quality copies could present a poor image of the organisation.

ACTIVITY

1 Find out which of the following advantages apply to: photocopiers; spirit copiers; and offset litho duplicators:

- Cheap for long runs
- Easy to use
- Clean
- Quick
- Gives good copies
- Has facilities such as
  - enlargement
  - reduction
  - auto feed
- Compact
- Quiet

2 If a photocopy costs 2p per sheet, a spirit copy costs 20p for a master and 1p a sheet, while an offset litho costs 50p for a master and 0.8p a sheet, which would you prefer to:

- Make three copies of a two-page memo for the boss?
- Make 5000 copies of an A5 sheet advertising the staff Christmas party?
- Make 50 copies of stock record sheets for the stationery?

Draw up a table to show what it would cost to make the copies using each of the three methods of copying.

Summary

1 *There are several ways to copy documents; for example, you can use a photocopier, a spirit copier, or an offset litho. You need to be cost-conscious when deciding how to copy documents.*

2 *You may be asked to make copies of confidential documents. You should not discuss the information with anyone.*

3 *Remember to pass the original documents back to the person who requested the copying to be done.*

4 *Never send poor quality copies out of the organisation because they will give a poor image. When using the photocopier you can use the contrast/darkness controls to get clear copies.*

LIAISING WITH CALLERS AND COLLEAGUES

12

This unit aims to:

- *Explain why you need to have good business relations with your colleagues, customers and clients.*
- *Identify ways in which an employer can help to make the organisation a pleasant place to work.*
- *Help you decide what you want to get out of a job.*
- *Gives some simple rules to help you get on well with colleagues, customers and clients.*

This unit is about getting on with people at work, both the people with whom you work and the customers or clients that you may have to meet.

Getting on with people at work

You spend a lot of time working. If you work a 40 hour week then you will probably spend nearly 2000 hours at work per year – so it is as well to get on with the people that you work with.

'I find people very easy to get on with here.'

Make a list of why you need to get on with people at work, e.g. makes going to work more enjoyable.

You should have been able to think of at least five reasons why it is important to get on with people for your own benefit. It is also important from your employer's point of view for a number of reasons:

- If staff do not get on well they will not work well together, causing jobs to take longer and mistakes to be made.
- If an organisation is not happy the staff may take sick leave regularly or move jobs quickly.
- The organisation can find it hard to get good staff if it has a reputation for being an unpleasant place to work.

As well as ensuring that staff are well paid an employer can help to make the organisation a pleasant place to work in by making sure that offices are:

- safe
- reasonably decorated
- kept at the right temperature
- well cleaned
- well lit

and by trying to give the staff all the resources needed to do their job. Many employers encourage staff associations, trips, competitions, etc. in order to make sure that their staff get on well with each other and enjoy work. Apart from what the employer does, what about you? What can you do to make sure that you get on with people at work?

Think about what you want from a place to work, like decent wages, a nice job and pleasant people to work with and then make a list. When you have done this try to put it into some sort of order with the most important points at the top. An example is included.

WHAT I WANT FROM WORK	HOW IMPORTANT IS IT?
A good wage	Fairly important No. 4

One thing to get clear at the start – do not expect to like everyone at work. There are some people who you will find hard work, probably the same people who will find you hard work. What you do have to do is to make an effort to get on with all the people that you work with. You may not like some people personally but you have to get on with them professionally. The same applies to customers and clients. It is important to show consideration and politeness to people, even if you are in a hurry, got out of bed the wrong side, have a headache or dislike them. There are a few simple rules to remember:

- If there is work to be shared out, take your share of it, including jobs like making drinks as well as the office work. No one likes to feel that they are doing your share – even if they do not say anything.
- If you are asked for information, or to do a job, do it as soon as you can. If you cannot do it, tell the person why and pass it on to someone who can, or hold the job until you can deal with it. Do not just ignore a job you cannot do at once – it only takes a minute to say 'I'll have to finish this for Miss Carr, then I can look that up for you. I'll give it to you in ten minutes, OK?'
- If you get information that someone else ought to know pass it on to them – do not wait for them to ask or make a mistake before you remember.
- If you need help ask. Doing a job wrong because you did not want to ask makes more work for everyone so it is better to ask if you are not sure.
- Be polite to people, say 'Hello' or 'Good morning' to them and make a point of saying goodbye when you go home. Take a few minutes to introduce yourself to colleagues who you have not met, especially if you have to deal with them as part of your work.
- If you are not good at remembering names make a list or draw a room plan with names on and keep it somewhere where you can look at it easily.
- If you really have problems working with someone, talk to them about it. You may find that you are doing a job in a way that makes their life difficult or that you could work something out with them to stop whatever the problem is. Remember; you do not have to like them, just get on with them. If talking to someone does not help then see your manager, staffing officer or personnel section – the sooner they are aware of a problem the sooner it can be solved.
- *Smile* at people – smiles are a much underrated way of getting things done in an organisation and it is difficult to say 'No' to someone who is smiling.
- Always be sensitive to other people's beliefs or values. What is important to them (e.g. their religion, culture, interests or hobbies) should always be respected. You may think them odd or amusing but never poke fun. After all, they may find some of your habits odd.

Make a list of five things that can annoy you when you have to work with someone. Assess whether they are real problems or whether you are just being fussy. If they really are a problem, suggest how it could be solved. For example, if you get annoyed by people who 'forget' their turn to make coffee at break you might suggest drawing up a rota or discreetly remind the offender a few minutes before his/her turn. You are not being fussy if people do not take their turn but it is not worth falling out over it and it can be settled with tact.

One thing is sure – the more pleasant and helpful you are to the people who you work with the more they are likely to respond in the same way to you.

Getting on with customers and clients

Customers and clients are the reason that you have a job. When you are dealing with a customer or client you represent the organisation. As far as that person is concerned, for the moment you are Shell, the Department of Social Security or Safeway. What you say to them and the way you treat them can make the difference between them being delighted and being furious. Why is it important that the customers are happy? Here are some of the reasons.

The customer is always right – sometimes deranged, misled, under a misapprehension, not fully in the picture or just plain round the bend. But always right.

- They will tell other people how good (or bad) you are and you will get more (or less) business as a result of it. The best advert you can have is a satisfied customer.
- A satisfied customer will probably come back to you again and repeat business is often the lifeblood of an organisation.
- It is a lot more pleasant to deal with happy customers than angry ones.

- Treating someone badly can make a minor complaint into a crusade for justice and they will move heaven and earth – making your life hard in the process.
- It is normally much easier to deal pleasantly with someone than to annoy them.

So, how do you keep clients happy? Although it depends on the situation there are a few general guidelines. If you deal with customers as part of your job you will probably be given special training on how to deal with them in your situation – selling, reception or complaints. Most organisations have their own rules and systems for dealing with customers and you are expected to stick to them – if you do not know what they are, ask your supervisor about them. But here are some general tips:

- Make sure that you greet people promptly. There is nothing worse than hanging round a reception desk or counter unsure of whether anyone has seen you or waiting for them to finish whatever they are doing. If you cannot attend to them at once, saying 'Good morning. I'll be with you in a moment' is better than ignoring them.
- Use people's names if you know them. Most people like to be called by their family or surname Mrs X or Ms Y – unless you know them well.

'Good morning, could I have your name please?'

'Yes, Joan Carter.'

'Thank you. Would you care to have a seat? Peter Cavendish will be right down, Mrs Carter.'

'Good morning, could I have your name please?'

'Yes, Joan Carter.'

'Thanks. Have a seat Joan – Peter Cavendish will be down in a moment.'

- It is usually better to start off with the more formal 'Mrs Carter' than to use first names. If they want you to use their first name they will tell you 'Oh, call me Joan.' If you are not sure whether to use Miss or Mrs and cannot see a wedding ring it is safest to use Ms.
- If people have to wait to see someone or for information to be found, try to talk to them – the chance to chat a bit relaxes people. If you cannot think of anything else try:
  - Is this your first visit here?
  - Did you manage to park all right?

- Would you like a coffee?
- Isn't the weather good/bad/changeable?

- If you cannot deal with someone, ask them to wait and pass the matter on to someone who can deal with it. Explain to the customer what you have done and why so that they do not think you are just ignoring them.
- If there are any delays or problems, explain the facts to the customer politely, keeping the reputation of the organisation in mind – 'We're waiting for a delivery' sounds better than 'We've run out.'

ACTIVITY

For the comments given below try to find a better way of saying what was said or dealing with the situation. An example is included:

WRONG	RIGHT
We've run out.	We are waiting for a delivery.
Haven't a clue, I'll try to find someone.	
We've lost the file.	
He's seeing someone important, have a seat and he'll be down when he can.	
There's no one here who knows anything about that.	
Joe's got that and I don't know where he's put it.	

Summary

1 *It is important to have good business relationships with people you work with and the organisation's clients and customers. Good relations make your job more pleasant and keep customers happy.*

2 *You can develop good business relations with people you work with in many ways, for example, by being considerate and polite, taking your share of the workload, passing*

on information, asking for help when you need it and being sensitive to other people's beliefs and values.

3 *If you have problems working with someone talk to them about it.*

4 *You can develop good business relations with customer and clients by responding to their needs. Be polite and courteous, greeting them promptly, finding out and using their names, explaining problems and difficulties to them.*

PROVIDING INFORMATION TO CUSTOMERS/CLIENTS

13

This unit aims to:

■ *Show you how to provide the information requested by customers and clients.*

This unit is about being able to inform customers about the products/services provided by your organisation and to give them the information that they need. When helping customers or clients they may have a specific question to ask, 'Does the LZ 40 model include a sheet feeder bin?' or want more general information, 'I'm looking for a new printer for my computer – what do you suggest?' Whatever the case you should be able to give them accurate, relevant and quick information or, if you cannot do so, pass them on to someone who can deal with the question with the minimum of delay.

'I know, choices are so hard to make.'

Depending on the type of business you will have different products and services that you offer – a small range of simple goods or a large range of complex goods or services. Whichever case is most like yours – and you may be somewhere in the middle – you need to be able to answer questions about the products/services on offer. This does not mean you have to know everything about all the goods/services but it is important to be able to answer the most common queries, to find more information fairly quickly, and to pass a query on if you are not able to answer it yourself.

When you are dealing with a customer/client they see you as the organisation that you work for. It is, therefore, important to give them the right impression and service. If you take the time and trouble to explain things to people and to tell them what is happening you will find them easier to deal with. Furthermore, if your organisation has to sell goods to survive, you need to get as many customers as you can to come back to you and to recommend you to their friends.

When providing information there are a number of stages to go through; not all of them may apply to all cases. It is up to you to choose and use them as appropriate:

1 Find out what the person wants to know.
2 Check that they can have the information they have asked for.
3 Provide the information or pass them on to someone who can help.
4 Help them to decide if the product or service is right for them.

1 Find out what the person wants to know

In order to find out what people want to know, you need to listen carefully, making sure that you have understood. Then you can either give them the information they need or pass them on to someone else who can help them.

If someone has a complex request or has a lot of information to give you, it is necessary to make a note of it so that you do not have to go back to ask 'What year did you say yours was?' Try to get all the information required to help you to provide the information that they want. It is easier and more efficient to ask for too much information to start with than to have to contact someone later to obtain more facts.

Keep the information that people tell you confidential if they ask you to – it is a good idea not to discuss what people tell you anyway unless it is meant to be common knowledge. 'That lady wants a toaster for her daughter's new flat' is acceptable. 'The bloke who's just left has got . . .' is not. If you are dealing with other firms they may tell you information they would not want their competitors to hear about – and you could lose a big contract if someone talks about customers to the wrong people.

2 Check they can have the information they have asked for

Check that the person is entitled to the information or goods. In some cases, such as where a firm offers help with running a piece of software after someone has bought it, they will only give help to those with the right identification. If this is the case, check how to make sure someone can be helped. Even if you cannot help, stay polite – they may be future customers.

When you are dealing with personal details, say in a personnel section or in a bank, you need to check very carefully that you are talking to the right person before you give out any information. Your organisation will probably have very strict rules about the sort of information that you can give out and you will need to find out what these are.

If your organisation stores information on computer you will have to be careful about the information that you give as the firm could be taken to court – and so could you – if you give information from a computer to someone who has no right to it.

3 Provide the information or pass them on to someone who can help

If there are any calculations to make (e.g. if someone wants to know how much more money some extras will cost on something that they have ordered) make sure that they are right before giving a firm price. If you cannot give a firm price, offer to write or phone back with the details as soon as you can get them. Do not just guess – the firm could be stuck with what you say.

Make sure that what you tell people is accurate. If you are not sure, then always *ask*. If you tell a customer something then the firm will probably have to stick to that – it could cost them a lot of money as well as possibly losing them a customer.

Make sure that what you say is relevant to the customer. There is no point telling someone how well a car behaves on the motorway if they are only interested in it for running around the town. Listen to what they want and describe the features of the product/service that will suit them rather than just telling them everything that you can remember about the product.

If you say that you will do something – do it; do not forget to send the catalogue/price list that you promised; remember to find a brochure of the model that you are getting in next week; pass the message on to the technical department and make sure they contact the customer.

If you have stocks of publicity material that you hand out to people make sure that you reorder stocks while you still have some left. Do not wait until you have actually run out of brochures before either reordering them or telling someone that the stocks are low.

Make sure that you keep any records up to date so that people know what has been said or given to a customer. At best it could be embarrassing for a sales representative to spend half an hour trying to sell a machine that you have already said will not suit the customer; at worst it could look as though you do not care about your customers – you just want to make sales.

4 Help them to decide if the product or service is right for them

Do not pressurise people – that probably loses more sales than it gains. Check after a time whether there is any information that the person needs or if there is anything that you can do to help.

ACTIVITY

Look at the conversations below. What could be improved in each case?

Wages section of a busy office. The phone rings . . .
Ann *Morning, wages section.*
Ian *Good morning. I've just got my payslip for this month. The problem is that the dog has chewed it and I don't know how much I've been paid of my overtime. Can you tell me the details?*
Ann *Hang on a minute I'll have to get them. Have you got your pay number?*
Ian *Sorry, I don't know it offhand. Look, my name's Ian Constable and I work in the finishing section – can't you find it from that?*
Ann *Yes. It'll take me a few minutes though. Can I call you back?*
Ian *No, it's all right. I'll hang on, love.*
Ann *OK, got it: Ian Constable. Your basic pay was the usual £915.30 and you got £198.25 in overtime. Do you want to know the tax and national insurance as well?*
Ian *No thanks. That's great. Bye.*

Reception area. Receptionist at desk, customer walks in . . .
Farzana *Good morning sir. Can I help you at all?*
Karl *I hope so; I'm looking for a fax machine for my office and the 590 model that you sell was recommended to me. What I need to know is whether it will work with my switchboard.*
Farzana *Oh. I don't really know much about the technical side, I only work in reception. Tell you what, I've got a brochure here – that might tell you about it. If that doesn't tell you I suppose I could try the engineers but they hate being disturbed at break time.*
Karl *Don't bother. I'll go somewhere else.*

Summary

1 *Customers need accurate and relevant information quickly.*

2 *You need to be able to answer customer queries about the products and services offered by your organisation.*

3 *Listen carefully and ask questions to find out what the customer wants to know and if*

there is a lot of information write it down so that you won't forget it.

4 If you cannot help a customer pass him on to someone who can.

5 Be careful who you give information to, some information is confidential and can only be given to specified people.

6 Ensure you have adequate stocks of publicity material to give to customers.

ASSIGNMENTS AND ACTIVITIES

14

This unit is designed to:

- *Give you practice in the clerical tasks.*
- *Provide a chance for you to use more than one competence at once, as you would have to do at work.*
- *Give you a chance to prove competence in some of the areas.*

ASSIGNMENT 1

Deecon Fashions

You work as an office clerk in the general office of Deecon Fashions, a medium-sized wholesalers, which buys and sells ladies' and gents' clothing. Today you have a range of tasks to do.

YOUR TASKS

1 Prepare index cards for the new customers and file the cards in geographical order ready to be inserted into the card index of customers.

2 Word process and print two copies of a memo concerning telephone skills training.

3 Write a letter to a new firm 'Belt Up' requesting a catalogue. Use a word processor. See the advert for the address. Print two copies of the letter.

4 From information provided calculate prices, enter data onto a spreadsheet and print out five copies of the data.

Information for Task 1

New customers of Deecon Fashions are:

Fashion World
Rigby Road
Manchester
MY1 7HJ
Tel: 061-874 6790
Contact: Mrs Sellers

Top Class Fashions
Willaby Street
Manchester
MS4 1JL
Tel: 061-903 8672
Contact: Mrs J. Cross

Accessories Galore
Derby Road
Preston
PV9 2GH
Tel: 0772 650989
Contact: Miss Langthorpe

Fashion Walk
King Street
Preston
JT8 3OP
Tel: 0772 980124
Contact: Jill Allen

Dress Style
Highbank Street
Blackburn
BY4 1HP
Tel: 0254 189111
Contact: Joan Luke

Easiwear Clothing
Dean Road South
Blackpool
BM4 5AL
Tel: 0253 758001
Contact: Mr Khan

Sadie's Fashions
Sutton Road
Preston
PR5 3GB
Tel: 0772 758122
Contact: Julie Smythies

High Class Clothes
Silverdale Street
Bolton
BK1 9HS
Tel: 0204 666401
Contact: Mrs Penfold

Jingle Jangle
South King Road
Manchester
MS7 2BB
Tel: 061-885 3100
Contact: Mr Crook

Tops and Bottoms
Preston Road
Blackburn
BS9 5NM
Tel: 0254 665012
Contact: Miss Kirby

Information for Task 2

Memo

Could you please type this for me asap. It's very urgent and must go out today. Thanks.

To PLEASE LEAVE BLANK

From Mr Morris, Training Officer

Date 10th Feb

Subject Telephone Skills Training

I hope you have settled into your new job and are enjoying your work at Deecon Fashions.

I have arranged a short training session on telephone skills at 2.30pm on 17th February for all new staff.

Please let me know if you are able to attend.

Information for Task 3

Belt Up

We manufacture a range of top quality fashion belts. Prices are competitive but no firm can compete with the style, design and exclusivity of our belts.

Send for a free catalogue or visit our warehouse –
Belt Up, Mintting Road North, Manchester MY60 2LN

Deecon Fashions, Whitesmiths Way, Manchester MY1 4WP

Information for Task 4

The company is preparing for a special promotion. From the details below calculate the new prices and enter the following details onto a spreadsheet: catalogue number, old price, price decrease %, new price. Print out five copies to be sent to sales representatives.

Catalogue No.	Old Price	Price decrease
0278645	£9.99	5%
84570938	£7.99	4%
73480126	£3.50	2%
158365/3	£6.00	5%
17648677	£10.85	8%

ASSIGNMENT 2

Bryan House – life as a receptionist

You work in a small guest house in the town of Wickery. The guest house is called Bryan House and caters for 25 guests. It has a first class restaurant which is open to the public. Bryan House is owned by Mr and Mrs Willows who manage the business. You are the receptionist.

As a receptionist you deal with a variety of work but your main duties include bookings and dealing with both resident guests and members of the public who come to the restaurant. You do a wide range of other tasks which you fit into your schedule when you are not busy.

YOUR TASKS

1 Deal appropriately with the callers. (It is intended that Task 1 is carried out as a role play but you would also learn from simply explaining how *you* would deal with the callers.)

2 Deal with the letters received, prepare letters confirming bookings, copy the letters and pre-sort the copy for filing.

Information for Task 1

The callers

Mr and Mrs Draycott come to the reception to hand in their keys and pay their bill as they are leaving today. You should give them their bill and take their keys. They tell you they are now travelling to Scotland to visit friends. When they see their bill they tell you it is wrong, you should check it and correct it if necessary.

Mr Johnson comes to the reception to hand in his keys and pay his bill as he is leaving today. You should prepare and give him his bill and take his keys. You took a telephone message for Mr Johnson this morning which you should explain to him.

A gentleman arrives and asks if you could let him have the home address of Mr and Mrs Draycott who were staying with you. The gentleman tells you that he met Mr and Mrs Draycott yesterday in one of the local pubs and they gave him their address so that he could visit them but unfortunately he lost it and does not want to lose contact with them.

Mr and Mrs Hill arrive with their two children. They have booked a family room. Unfortunately there has been a mistake with the booking and they have been booked into a double room. All your family rooms are already booked out.

Mr and Mrs Douglas ask where the tourist information centre is so that they can get some information about the town.

A young person telephones to ask if you cater for wedding parties. The wedding is in February. They need to know about costs.

Mrs Buxton, who is staying at the guest house asks if you can direct her to the railway station.

A policeman arrives to ask whether you have seen a particular man and shows you a photograph of the gentleman who you are sure was the one who asked you for the address of Mr and Mrs Draycott.

BOOKINGS BOOK		BRYAN HOUSE								WEEK COMMENCING. Sat 6 March
ROOM	VISITORS	TARIFF for Bed & Breakfast	SAT 6th	SUN 7th	MON 8th	TUE 9th	WED 10th	THU 11th	FRI 12th	NOTES
1	Mr & Mrs Draycott	£15 per person per day	Arrive 6pm X	X	Dep am X					Arrive Sat pm Dep Mon am
2	Mr Johnson	£15 per day	Arrive 7pm X	X	Dep am X					"
3	Mrs Buxton & fam	£15 per adult £10 p.child		X	X	X	X	X		Arrive Sunday am about 9 am
4	Mrs Pollock	£15 per day	X	X	X	X				
5										
6										

MESSAGE FOR

Mr _Johnson — Room 2_

WHILE YOU WERE OUT

M _Helen_

Of _____

Telephone No _____

Telephoned	✓	Please ring	
Called to see you		Will call again	
Wants to see you		Urgent	

Message: _She will meet you at the_
railway station at 4.30 pm today
as you requested.

Date _Mon 8th March_ Time _8.05am_

Received by _Receptionist_

Mr and Mrs Draycott's bill

GUEST: Mr & Mrs Draycott Room no: 1	**BRYAN HOUSE**			Date: Mon 8 Mar
Persons	Service	Tariff	Days	Total
2	Bed & breakfast	15.00	3	90.00
	Bed, breakfast & evening meal			
	Extras: Tea Coffee Lunch			
	Sub total			90.00
	Add VAT at 17.5%			15.75
	TOTAL AMOUNT DUE			105.75

Mr Johnson's bill for completion

GUEST: Room no:	**BRYAN HOUSE**			Date:	
Persons	Service	Tariff	Days	Total	
	Bed & breakfast				
	Bed, breakfast & evening meal				

	Extras: Tea
	      Coffee
	      Lunch				

	Sub total				
	Add VAT at 17.5%				
	TOTAL AMOUNT DUE				

Information for Task 2

You open the mail to find the letters on pp 134–5. Each of the guests has written to you previously to enquire if there are vacancies at Bryan House from Friday 28 to Monday 31 August, which is a bank holiday weekend. You have sent a letter to say that you had vacancies available and that they should send you a deposit of £10 per person if they wished to book accommodation. The tariff for the bank holiday weekend is £60 per person. The letters which you have just opened are in response to your letter.

You should prepare letters of confirmation for Mrs Willows to sign. You should use a word processor to make a standard letter, copy it three times and insert appropriate details. Print two copies, one to be sent and one to file. Pre-sort the file copies by putting them in alphabetical order.

Letters – house rules

1 Letters should have a fully blocked layout.
2 Since you know who you are writing to, use 'Yours sincerely' or 'Yours' for a regular client.
3 Letters should have a friendly tone.
4 A copy of letters sent to clients is always kept.
5 On copies of letters of confirmation always underline the name of the client, the dates they require, their room and service requirments.

54 Barrington Way
High Burn Rd South
off Ryburn St
Oxford

6 March 19--

Dear Mr Willows

We have enclosed a cheque for
£30 to confirm our booking of a
room with a double and a
single bed from Friday 28th to
Monday 31st August.

We look forward to seeing
you again

Regards to Mrs Willows.

Yours

Sam Hill

28 Spindley Gardens
YORK
YO1 9RL

5 March 19--

Dear Mr Willows

Thank you for your letter which I received today.

I would like to confirm our booking for 28-31 August
and enclose a cheque for £20.

If possible, could we have a room at the front of
the house?

Thank you again.

Yours sincerely

Mrs Walters

Mrs Walters

263 Sideley St
Bridgeway
LANDLEY
LY17 3RN

6th March 19--

Dear Mr Willows

Thank you for your letter.

We are very pleased that you have vacancies for the
Bank Holiday weekend of 28th-31st August.

I have enclosed a cheque for £50 as the deposit for
our booking. We require one double room for my
husband and myself, and one room for the three girls.

We expect to arrive at 10 am. We look forward to
staying at Bryan House again.

Yours

Mrs Paxton

Mrs R Paxton

PS We really had a super time when we stayed at
Christmas and hope to book for next year. Thank
you again.

---

18 Stallbank Rd
Sandybank
Pollington
BF3 4TL

5th March 19--

Dear Mr Willows

We have enclosed a cheque for £20 for our double
room for 28th-31st August.

We hope you are well and look forward to our
stay.

Yours sincerely

Jim & Jackie Hill

Mr and Mrs J Hill

ASSIGNMENT 3

Best Choice

You are a clerk in a general office of Best Choice, a retailer selling children's clothing. As part of your job you deal with petty cash and process invoices for payment.

YOUR TASKS

1 **Write up the petty cash book for the week commencing Monday 11 April. The imprest amount is £60.**

2 **Process invoices for payment.**

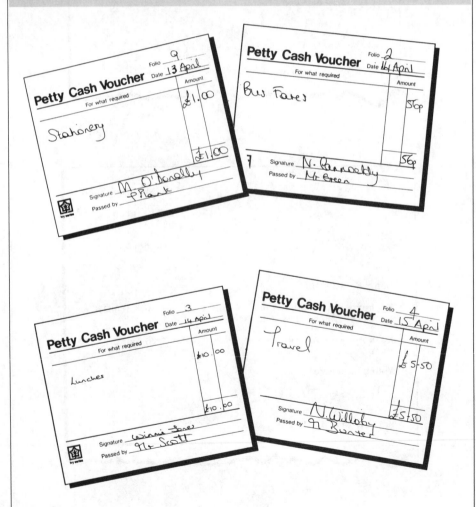

PETTY CASH ACCOUNT							BEST CHOICE	
Cash rec £	Date	Details	Voucher	Total paid £	Travel £	Postage £	Food £	Sundries £
60·00	14 Apr	Balance						

Information for Task 1

Petty cash transactions

Monday: You receive petty cash vouchers 1, 2, 3
Tuesday: You receive petty cash vouchers 4, 5, 6
Wednesday: You receive petty cash voucher no. 7
Thursday: You receive petty cash voucher no. 8
Friday: You receive petty cash vouchers 9, 10

Information for Task 2

Passing an invoice for payment – house rules

If you pass the invoice for payment write 'Passed for Payment' on the invoice and you should date and initial the invoices.

If the invoice cannot be passed for payment then complete and attach a problem card (see example below) to the appropriate invoice explaining why the invoice cannot be passed for payment.

PROBLEM CARD
This invoice cannot be passed for payment because:

Orders placed

This letter was received from Rawcliffe Printers. In response to the letter you place a telephone order. Read the letter and telephone conversation following.

```
                     Rawcliffe Printers
            26 Hall St, FINLEY, Surrey GU12 6JR

                                    Date: 27 March --

Best Choice
118 Bellshaw Rd
Finley
Surrey GU12 3TU

Dear Sir/Madam

Rawcliffe Printers are offering you a very special
deal. We can design and print your business stationery
for the special price of £300.

The special pack on offer consists of artwork, 3000
letterheads and 3000 business cards.

You are invited to take advantage of this special offer
by placing an order on or before 10 April.

Yours faithfully

Maxine Delaney

Maxine Delaney
Manager
```

Telephone order placed on 7 April.

Rawcliffe Printers *Rawcliffe Printers, good morning.*

Best Choice *Good morning, I have just received a letter from you giving details of a special offer for 3000 business cards, letterheads and artwork. We would like to place an order but we don't need the artwork as we can send you the letterhead and business card we use.*

Rawcliffe Printers *That's fine, could you please give me your name and the name and address of the business please.*

Best Choice *Yes, of course. My name is Penny Sinclair and the business is Best Choice, 118 Bellshaw Rd, Finley, Surrey GU12 3TU*

Rawcliffe Printers *Right, Penny Sinclair, Best Choice, 118 Bellshaw Rd, Finley Surrey GU12 3TU. If you send me the letterhead and card we will be able to deliver straight away.*

Best Choice *Great, but there is just one thing. Since we are not needing artwork, could we have a reduction on the price, please.*

Rawcliffe Printers *If you would like to wait a minute please I'll ask the manager . . . Yes, we can give you a £30 reduction. Is that OK?*

Best Choice *That's great. Thank you, goodbye.*

Rawcliffe Printers *Thank you, goodbye.*

BEST CHOICE
118 Bellshaw Rd, Finley
Surrey GU12 3TU

Order No. 05132

To: Kiddie Wear
Kingsway Industrial Estate
Surrey

Date: Mon 5 April --

Quantity	Item	Unit Price	Total
100	Warm Winter Woollies	5 . 00	500 - 00
50	Girls Fuzzy Jumpers	5 . 50	275 - 00

BEST CHOICE
118 Bellshaw Rd, Finley
Surrey GU12 3TU

Order No. 05159

To: Surrey Office Equipment Ltd
Lambeth Industrial Est
Surrey

Date: Mon 5 April --

Quantity	Item	Unit Price	Total
1	TS110 Printer	200 - 00	200 - 00
20	Printer Ribbons	4 - 50	90 - 00
35	Calculators	5 - 00	175 - 00

Invoices received

KIDDIEWEAR

INVOICE

To: Best Choice
118 Bellshaw Road
Finley Surrey GU12 3TU

No.

| Date | Your order | 05132 | Terms | 5% trade discount |
| 14/4/-- | Despatch date | | Carriage | |

Quantity	Ref	Description	Unit price	Total price		VAT rate
100		Warm winter woollies	5.00	500	00	
50		Girls' fuzzy jumpers	5.50	275	00	

Gross value	775	00
Discount	38	75
VAT		
Total net value	£736	25

RAWCLIFFE PRINTERS
36 Hall Street, Finley
Surrey GU12 6JR

INVOICE

To: Best Choice
    118 Bellshaw Road
    Finley Surrey GU12 3TU   No. 823

Date	Your order		Terms	
14/4/--	Despatch date		Carriage	

Quantity	Ref	Description	Unit price	Total price		VAT rate
		For design and supply of business stationery		£300	00	

Gross value		
Discount		
VAT		
Total net value	£300	00

SURREY OFFICE EQUIPMENT
Lambeth Industrial Estate
Surrey S16 1RV

INVOICE

To: Best Choice
118 Bellshaw Road
Finley Surrey GU12 3TU   No. 0311/2

Date	Your order	Terms	2.5% 28 days
14/4/--	Despatch date	Carriage	

Quantity	Ref	Description	Unit price	Total price		VAT rate
		1 TS110 Printer		200	00	17.5
		20 Printer Ribbons		90	00	17.5
		35 Calculators		175	00	17.5
		Gross value		465	00	
		Discount				
		VAT		81	37	
		Total net value		546	37	

SHINY SHOP FITTINGS
P.O. Box 82
Manchester M74 5QN

INVOICE

To: Best Choice
     118 Bellshaw Road
     Finley Surrey GU12 3TU

No. 1326/5

Date	Your order		Terms 2.5% 28 days
11/4/--	Despatch date		Carriage

Quantity	Ref	Description	Unit price	Total price		VAT rate
		Supply of metal trim for designer range shop fittings		£32	00	

Gross value		
Discount		
VAT		
Total net value	£32	00

Deliveries received

GOODS RECEIVED   **Date** 10 April

SUPPLIER: Surrey Office Equipment
GOODS RECEIVED: 1 TS110 printer
                                      20 Printer ribbons
                                      35 Calculators

GOODS RECEIVED   **Date** 11 April

SUPPLIER: Kiddie Wear
GOODS RECEIVED: 100 Warm winter woollies
                                      50 Girls' fuzzy jumpers

SUPPLIER: Rawcliffe Printers
GOODS RECEIVED: Business stationery:
                                      3000 letterheads
                                      3000 business cards

ASSIGNMENT 4

Greetings Ltd

Greetings Ltd manufactures and distributes cards, wrapping paper, party hats, masks and Christmas decorations to retail shops.

You work as an office junior in the accounts department at the head office.

YOUR TASKS

1 Record the post delivered to the accounts department.

2 Keep records of office stocks in the department.

3 Check calculations.

4 Input data into the computer.

Information for Task 1

The organisation of the accounts department

The accounts department is divided into various sections:

- *Debtors section:* responsible for obtaining payment from the customers of Greetings Ltd.
- *Creditors section:* responsible for payment of bills.
- *Costing section:* responsible for costing products and analysing income and expenditure.

In addition there is:

- an office manager (Susan McKenna)
- an assistant manager (Simon Davison)
- an office junior

Greetings Ltd. Distributing mail within departments – house rules

1 Pass mail marked personal or confidential to the appropriate person unopened.
2 Record mail received by the department in the mail received book.
3 Check enclosures are present and are stapled to the main document.

Mail received

1 A letter addressed as follows:

CONFIDENTIAL

       Ms Susan McKenna
       Accounts Office Manager
       Head Office
       Greetings Ltd
       Runshaw Avenue
       Newton
       N23 81K

---

2 An invoice (no 80/1125) from Catering Equipment Ltd, Bassmill Cross, Newton N11 1RL for the repair of Industrial F1800 Dishwasher – parts and labour costing £350.

3 An envelope containing the following letter:

F G Paper Ltd
Distributors of top quality paper
Asburne Rd, Newton N12 3RT

Date: 16 Dec--

Greetings Ltd
Runshaw Avenue
Newton N23 81K

Dear Sir/Madam,

According to our records invoice number 06213 requesting payment of £380 is still outstanding.

This is the third request for payment. If payment is not made within 14 days we will have no alternative but to put the matter in the hands of our solicitors.

Yours faithfully,

S Strutt
Manager

Mail Received Book		
Date	Sender	Receiver
Mon 16 December	A T Electrical	Creditors section
"	Confidential	S McKenna
"	Styles & Sons Ltd	Debtors section
Tues 17 December	Mr Huntington internal memo.	Costings section
"	The office shop	Creditors section
"	Card and Paper Co	Creditors section
"	Cards & candles	Debtors section

Information for Task 2

Stock control in the office – house rules

1 The stock cupboard should always be kept locked when not in use.

2 Each item of stock has a code number. Any new item is given the next available number.

3 Each item has a stock record card which must be updated when goods are issued or received.

4 The stock record cards are filed in numerical order.

5 Stock is reordered when the level of stock reaches the reorder level shown on the stock record card. Orders are listed on the order sheet.

6 The order sheet is collected fortnightly.

Stock issued on Wednesday 18 December

3 bottles of liquid paper	1 box staples
1 notepad	5 ball point pens

Stock received on Wednesday 18 December

50 notepads
10 bottles of liquid paper
8 printer ribbons

Stock record cards to be updated

ITEM: Liquid Paper 06
SUPPLIER: AD Office Supplies
REORDER LEVEL: 10
REORDER QUANTITY: 30

DATE	RECEIVED	ISSUED	BALANCE
9 Dec			9
13 Dec		1	8

A

ITEM: Note pads 11
SUPPLIER: AD Office Supplies
REORDER LEVEL: 20
REORDER QUANTITY: 50

DATE	RECEIVED	ISSUED	BALANCE
29 Nov		2	20
10 Dec		5	15
14 Dec		2	13

B

ITEM: Staples 13
SUPPLIER: AD Office Supplies
REORDER LEVEL: 10 boxes
REORDER QUANTITY: 30 boxes

DATE	RECEIVED	ISSUED	BALANCE
6 Dec			8
7 Dec	30		38
10 Dec		1	37
13 Dec		2	35

C

ITEM: Ball-point pens 18
SUPPLIER: AD Office Supplies
REORDER LEVEL: 20
REORDER QUANTITY: 100

DATE	RECEIVED	ISSUED	BALANCE
7 Dec			41
7 Dec		1	40
8 Dec		6	34
13 Dec		10	24

D

ITEM: Rubbers 19
SUPPLIER: AD Office Supplies
REORDER LEVEL: 10
REORDER QUANTITY: 30

DATE	RECEIVED	ISSUED	BALANCE
29 Nov		1	10
6 Dec		2	8
7 Dec	30		38

E

ITEM: Printer ribbons 20
SUPPLIER: Computer ware
REORDER LEVEL: 4
REORDER QUANTITY: 8

DATE	RECEIVED	ISSUED	BALANCE
9 Dec			4
13 Dec		1	3

F

ORDER SHEET
ACCOUNTS DEPARTMENT

Orders will be placed on .... 20 Dec ....

ITEM	CODE	QUANTITY	SUPPLIER
Paper clips	01	20 boxes	AD Office Supplies
Calculator batteries	02	60	AD Office Supplies
Index cards	07	10 packs	AD Office Supplies

Information for Tasks 3 and 4

You are given monthly sales figures for cards for the month of November last year and this year. The percentage increase or decrease has been calculated.

You have been asked to check the percentage increase or decrease figures and make any corrections required. Then input the data into the computer and print out suitable graphs and charts showing:

1 The increase or decrease in total sales of cards in November.
2 The increase or decrease in

■ Christmas cards   ■ Birthday cards

SALES ANALYSIS
PRODUCT: CARDS
MONTH: NOVEMBER

Type of card	Last year £	This year £	% increase + % decrease −
Christmas	28 000	36 500	30.5%+
Birthday: Father	2 000	2 500	20%+
Mother	6 000	8 000	33.33%+
Sister	2 000	1 000	100%−
Brother	1 000	1 500	50%+
Children	6 000	5 000	20%−
Other	8 000	10 000	25%+

ASSIGNMENT 5

Ainscough Insurance Services

Ainscough Insurance Services Ltd is a large organisation which deals with all aspects of private and commercial insurance. It has a head office in Ribbottom and branches throughout the country.

You work at the head office in the accounts department as a VDU operator/clerk.

The company is offering a new service to clients by allowing them to pay their annual premium by 12 monthly installments by direct debit.

YOUR TASKS

1 **Prepare copies and complete standard letters to be sent to clients whose policy needs renewing.**

2 **Update computer records.**

3 **Send bank instructions to the banks.**

4 **Pre-sort documents for filing.**

POLICY RENEWALS

Policy No.	C70003888, Name: F Graye
Address:	52 Loghouse Lane, Lostock Place, Pouldene, PF1 9AG
Annual Premium:	£280
Renewal date:	7th July
Policy No.	H00835411, Name: Angela Proudfoot
Address:	17 Chaple Street, Wycombe, WD7 4RN
Annual Premium:	£226
Renewal date:	8th July

Ainscough Insurance Services
Alfred Street, Ribbottom RB2 4VL

Dear . . . .

Re Policy No . . . .

As you know your premium is due on . . . .

We are now introducing a system whereby you can pay your insurance premium of . . . . by installments.

Should you wish to take advantage of this service the payments would be paid by direct debit which is organised by you simply completing and returning the tear off slip below.

The installments would be 12 equal monthly payments of . . . .

We hope you will be able to take advantage of this new service.

Yours faithfully,

K D Sadler
Accounts Manager

BANK INSTRUCTION

Name of Bank_____

I hereby authorise you to pay direct debits from my account at the request of Ainscough Insurance Services Ltd.

Account name: _____

Bank address: _____

Account no: _____ (8 digits)

Sort code: _____

Signature: _____

POLICY NUMBER _____

Total Premium _____

Installment amount _____

Renewal date _____

Preparation for Task 2

Before you attempt Task 2 you need to create a database and enter details of six clients. The information for this is given below.

The file created should look like this:

Policy No:
Client Name:
Client Address:

Installment Amount:
Renewal Date:

Bank Details
Account Name:
Account No:
Bank Name:
Bank Address:

Sort Code No:

Once you have created your files then input the following details for six clients.

Policy No: H0005678
Client Name: Paul Howard
Client Address: 15 Turnpike Lane, Badlington, B19 5YG

Policy No: H1562621
Client Name: A Patel
Client Address: 39 Tavington Terr., Whittington, WH8 3KA

Policy No: H5210078
Client Name: Mrs J Howard
Client Address: Orchard Way, Carrington, CE4 6MX

Policy No: C6210050
Client Name: Deecon Fashions
Client Address: Whitesmith's Way, Manchester, MY1 4WP

Policy No: C2012159
Client Name: Joseph Adams
Client Address: Willoby St, Preston, PR9 2CC

Policy No: C8052217
Client Name: Annie Wilding
Client Address: Park House, Mount Rd, Siddleton, SP8 7BV

Information for Task 2

Two weeks ago the six clients in your database were sent the standard letter telling them about the payment by direct debit. They have returned the tear-off slip as they wish to take advantage of payment by direct debit. You now need to update their records on your database.

Some clients do not complete the forms fully and, therefore, where there is insufficient information given on the bank instruction you need to send the client a letter requesting him/her to complete the required details.

BANK INSTRUCTION

Name of Bank _____ Barnley Bank _____

I hereby authorise you to pay direct debits from my account at the request of Ainscough Insurance Services Ltd.

Account Name: P. Howard

Bank Address: Lovatt St, Badlington

Account No: 13586404   (8 digits)

Sort Code: 18 21 06

Signature: P. Howard

POLICY NUMBER   H0005678

Total Premium   £256

Installment Amount   £21.33

Renewal Date   18th June

BANK INSTRUCTION

Name of Bank ___ Norland Bank ___

I hereby authorise you to pay direct debits from my
account at the request of Ainscough Insurance Services
Ltd.

Account Name: ___ A & J Howard ___

Bank Address: ___ Lord St, Carrington ___

Account No: ___ 26642134 ___ (8 digits)

Sort Code: ___ 10 18 51 ___

Signature: ___ A Howard ___

POLICY NUMBER ___ H5210078 ___ Installment Amount ___ £25 ___

Total Premium ___ £300 ___ Renewal Date ___ 17 June ___

BANK INSTRUCTION

Name of Bank ___ Norland Bank ___

I hereby authorise you to pay direct debits from my
account at the request of Ainscough Insurance Services
Ltd.

Account Name: ___ A Wilding ___

Bank Address: ___ Church St, Siddleton ___

Account No: ___ (8 digits)

Sort Code: ___

Signature: ___ A. Wilding ___

POLICY NUMBER ___ C8052217 ___ Installment Amount ___ £19.17 ___

Total Premium ___ £230 ___ Renewal Date ___ 16 June ___

BANK INSTRUCTION

Name of Bank ___Banley Bank___

I hereby authorise you to pay direct debits from my account at the request of Ainscough Insurance Services Ltd.

Account Name: ___Miss A Patel___

Bank Address: ___Denelle St, Whittington___

Account No: ___67067119___ (8 digits)

Sort Code: ___52 11 01___

Signature: ___a Patel___

POLICY NUMBER ___H1562621___   Installment Amount ___£15.83___

Total Premium ___£190___   Renewal Date ___15 June___

BANK INSTRUCTION

Name of Bank ___Royal Higgs Bank___

I hereby authorise you to pay direct debits from my account at the request of Ainscough Insurance Services Ltd.

Account Name: ___Deecon Fashions___

Bank Address: ___Park Rd, Manchester___

Account No: ___55110281___ (8 digits)

Sort Code: ___14 31 09___

Signature: ___G M Clark.___

POLICY NUMBER ___C6210050___   Installment Amount ___£48.33___

Total Premium ___£580___   Renewal Date ___18 June___

BANK INSTRUCTION

Name of Bank ___Royal Higgs Bank___

I hereby authorise you to pay direct debits from my account at the request of Ainscough Insurance Services Ltd.

Account Name: ___Joseph Adams___

Bank Address: ___Waterloo Rd, Preston___

Account No: ___52011119___ (8 digits)

Sort Code: ___12 22 33___

Signature: ___Joseph Adams___

POLICY NUMBER ___C2012159___

Total Premium ___£180___

Installment Amount ___£15___

Renewal Date ___18 June___

Preparation for Task 3

Pre-task

Input the following letter on a word processor.

AINSCOUGH INSURANCE SERVICES LTD
ALFRED STREET
RIBBOTTOM RB2 4VL

Manager of
Bank Name
(Bank Address)

(Date)

Dear Sir/Madam

Our client has requested to pay their insurance premium by direct debit. Please comply with the attached instructions.

Yours faithfully,

K D Sadler
Accounts Manager

Information for Task 3

When a client has correctly completed the bank instruction form and you have updated your database you should:

1 Prepare a letter for the client's bank (by putting the name and address of the client's bank on the above letter).
2 Print two copies of the letter (one for the bank and one to file).
3 Attach one letter to a copy of the Bank Instruction ready to be sent to the bank.

Information for Task 4

Pre-sort your copy of the letters to the banks ready for filing. They are filed in alphanumerical order.

This set of units aims to:

- *Present a good image of yourself when applying for jobs.*
- *Help you to understand how you fit into an organisation and explain your rights and responsibilities at work.*
- *Explain the need to use resources carefully and how to avoid waste.*
- *Explain the importance of the organisation having a good image and how you can contribute to this.*
- *Explain how to keep customers happy and how to deal with difficult customers.*
- *Provide you with the chance to practise Work Role competencies and some of the Clerical Tasks in Business Support Systems.*

Performing your role at work

This section of the book will look at how you fit into a business and consider the rights and responsibilities that you have when you are at work. It is split into a number of units with activities included and there is also a unit of assignments for you to work through.

FINDING A JOB AND KNOWING YOUR RIGHTS

This unit is designed to:

- *Explore the reasons why people work.*
- *Take you through the process of getting a job.*
- *Explain your rights and responsibilities at work.*

Why do people work? There are all sorts of reasons for working. Make a list of the reasons and put them in order of importance to you. There are no right or wrong answers because everyone has their own set of priorities – though money will probably be one of everyone's priorities. An example is included.

REASON	HOW IMPORTANT
Money	Very (1)
To keep busy	Quite (5)

You will probably have come up with quite a few reasons for working and at the top of the list you may have the same few as some other people if you compare your list with theirs. The most common reasons that people give for working are:

- To make a living.
- So as not to be bored.
- To be with people and make friends.
- Because they enjoy the job they do.

For most people there will be a mix of reasons for working, like the two below:

Tom   *I can't really say that I took this job for the money because it doesn't pay that much – it's not that it's badly paid, just that I could probably make more at some other places. What I like is that I get the chance to be my own boss a bit and they give me a lot of responsibility. Another thing is that it's a really nice place to work – I get on well with everyone and you can ask people for help if you need it, they'll all pitch in if there's a rush right from Leroy, he's the boss, down to Eddie who comes in for a few hours in the afternoon to help with the deliveries. Also they trust you. I went to Leroy soon after I started to ask for a half day off and I was really nervous about it. The last place I worked they would've wanted seven reasons and made it into a big thing; Leroy just said, 'Fine, Tom, no problem, thanks for letting me know' – he knew I'd catch up the work and I did by coming in early for the next week.*

Jenny   *'Money. That's the main thing in this job for me. I work really hard and I make a good wage here. I need the money because I'm getting married soon and we want the deposit for a house and we'll have to buy furniture and all that. It's not a difficult job but it can get a bit boring and you don't have much of a chance to talk to people when the machines are on. Most of the people here are OK though I only really know a few of them who go on the same breaks as me. It's really handy for me as well because I can get the train from near home to the station just down the road and the times work in well; I finish at 4 in the afternoon and I can just catch the 4.11 which gets me home for 4.30.*

ACTIVITY

Make a list of Tom's reasons for working and Jenny's reasons for working in order of importance to them.

Over time people's reasons for working can change. Jenny needs money for a house, furniture and getting married. Once she has her home set up she might want a job that she enjoys more and be less concerned about making as much money as possible. Tom, who needs money to live, but is not bothered about making the most money he can might find in a few years that he needs to make more money to set up in business for himself. You will have your own reasons for working now, and they may change in the future.

Which of the following statements do you think apply to you? Discuss them with another student and compare your views.

'I work to live. I don't live to work.'

'I want a job I enjoy. As long as I get enough money to get by that'll do me.'

'The people you work with are more important than what you do.'

'As long as it's legal I'll do the job that makes the most cash.'

'I want a job that lets me be my own boss a bit. I don't want to be a robot.'

'I want a job that'll let me get on, not some dead end.'

Where can you work?

Whatever reasons you have for working you will need a job to work in – it could be working for yourself or, as most people do, working for someone else. There are all sorts of organisations who need people to do office work:

- businesses, both large and small
- charities
- government departments
- local authorities
- voluntary organisations
- trade unions
- clubs.

The list could go on, but these are some of the main ones.

Quite often people choose where to work on the grounds that they like the sound of the job, or that they will find the place convenient to work at, or because of the rate of pay. Sometimes they do not look closely at what sort of organisation it is until they go to the interviews or start work there. There are three main types of organisation that you could work for:

1 the public sector organisation
2 the private sector organisation.

1 The public sector

Organisations run by the government or local authorities. The main public sector organisations include the following.

- **Local authorities** have jobs in all sorts of departments to help run the district. The departments include collecting local taxes, organising services like parks and sports centres, helping to keep track of planning and building, and promoting the area to businesses and individuals. If you work for a local authority there will probably be a chance of getting day release to study for qualifications and there may be jobs that you could be promoted to in time. The local authority will probably also be responsible for jobs in places like schools and children's homes. Your local county or town hall probably has more office jobs than anyone else in the area.

■ **The Civil Service** has jobs in all sorts of government departments like benefit offices, tax offices and job centres. Working for the civil service gives you a chance to be promoted and to work your way up through the department you work in. You will be encouraged to study for qualifications at college and, if you ever have to move you may be able to transfer to another area without having to find a new job.

■ There are a few other organisations in the public sector as well that you could get a job with such as the health service (the biggest employer in Europe), British Rail, the Atomic Energy Authority or the Sports Council. These belong to the government but tend to be run as organisations on their own.

2 The private sector

The private sector includes businesses owned by individuals or groups of people. It has all sorts of businesses in it from one person businesses and small shops through to very big companies like Shell, McDonalds or Rover. Businesses in the private sector will employ people to do all sorts of office jobs and the jobs can be very important depending on where you work. Below is a list showing what you might find in different businesses and the views of some typical employees:

BUSINESS	WHAT IS THE JOB LIKE	WHAT DO YOU GET?
1 Small firm	You will probably have a wide range of things to do and the chance to sort out your own day a lot. Not much chance of promotion.	Wages Get to know people Variety Can be flexible as to time

'I work doing the office side for the newsagency on the Parade. There's only me doing the books and that so I get a lot of freedom to do things my way. Helen lets me come in at 9.30 after I've seen the kids off to school and I go in time to pick them up in the afternoon and take some work home. I'd hate to work in a big office.'

2 Medium firm	You will probably work in an office with other people and might have the chance of promotion. You will not get to do as many different jobs as in a smaller firm.	Wages Company Perks like staff discounts Regular times

'There are six of us in the office here. I do most of the sales side and work a lot with Anwar who does the invoicing. It's nice to work in an office where you get to know people and you can all pitch in if there's a problem. It's handy getting 5% discount as well.'

3 Big firm	You will probably do a very specific job in a big office with a lot of others. You can get to know a particular job well. Training tends to be good.	Wages Perks like cheap meals and discounts Good sick pay Help to study for qualifications

'This place has a lot of staff; I don't really know how many work here – hundreds I guess. I input changes in customer files onto the computer and send out revised details to the branch offices. The job is very technical and I had three weeks' training before I started. We've got a cheap canteen here and a sports club that we can use free and, after five years, we get an extra ten days holiday per year.'

ACTIVITY

What sort of place would you like to work in? Make a note of what you think the good points and the bad points are of working for small, medium and big firms and then try to decide which you think would be the best for you.

Finding a job

Wherever you want to work you need to find a suitable job for you, apply for it and get it. This section will give you some help.

When looking for work you need to find out where the sort of jobs that you want will be advertised and how you can find them. Some of the main places to look for jobs are:

- job centres
- local papers
- employment agencies
- in firms and offices themselves.

You can also write to firms direct asking them if they have any vacancies or if they will have any in the near future. This is quite expensive in terms of your time and postage but can be worthwhile if you want a particular job because firms may be impressed by your taking the initiative and trouble to write to them.

When you have found what you want you will have to go through the process of applying for the job. The flow chart illustrated outlines the stages and the forms/documents that you will need.

STAGE	FORMS/DOCUMENTS
Find job to apply for	**Job advert**
Send or phone for details	**Job description**
	Details of the business
Complete application form	**Application form**
or letter of application	**Letter of application**
	Curriculum vitae
either	
Letter to say you have not got the job	
or	
Letter asking you to go for interview for the job	
Interview	**Proof of qualifications**
either	
Letter to say you have not got the job	**Job offer letter**
or	
Offer of the job	
Accept job	**Acceptance letter**
Start work	

Fig 15.1 Applying for a job

Getting details of the job

Usually when you ask for details of a job you will be sent details about the firm, details of the pay and conditions and details about the actual job.

The way these are presented varies from firm to firm but you will probably get some sort of job description which tells you about the job.

Job description

Post: trainee marketing assistant

The job is at our Poulton site and is based on a 35-hour week. Pay is on the scales you have been given a copy of. The main jobs involved are:

- helping with the preparation of the advertising produced by the section
- general office duties including filing, copying and some data input work
- attending exhibitions and helping set up exhibitions
- booking transport, accommodation and facilities for staff in the section
- issuing and maintaining records of office stock and of promotional material
- any other duties as may reasonably form a part of the work of the section.

This job description tells you what you will be doing in the job and will help you to decide if you would like the job and be good at it. It cannot give you all the detail that you might like such as what sort of people you would be working with or what the office is like but it does help you decide whether to apply or not.

Applying for the job

If you like the sound of the job after reading the information you have been given you may decide to apply for the job. If you do, the application is the only criterion they will have to judge you on – a good application may give you an interview, a bad one may stop you getting one. There are a number of different types of application firms may ask for:

1 send a curriculum vitae
2 write a letter of application
3 complete an application form.

and you may be asked to use a combination of these. Each of these ways of applying for a job requires a lot of care and thought if you are going to convince the firm you are worth an interview. It is only if you get an interview that you will get the chance to convince them that you are the right person for the job.

1 Send a curriculum vitae

A **curriculum vitae** (cv) is a short history of your life like the one given below.

Curriculum vitae

Personal details

Name:	John Robin NORTH
Address:	17 Constable Grove
	Leighton
	BLACKBURN
	BB2 7SR
Telephone:	(0254) 510798
Date of birth:	29 May 1970

Education

1975–81	Heathford Primary School, Blackburn
1981–6	Leighton School, Leighton, Blackburn
1986–7	Blackburn College, Blackburn

Qualifications

1986	Five CSE passes: Mathematics grade 1, English grade 2, French grade 2, History grade 3, Biology grade 3.
1987	BTEC First Diploma in Business and Finance

Work experience

1984–6	Carter & Son, Leighton, Blackburn. Part time leaflet delivery, also worked in the office for the summer in 1986.
1986–7	McDonalds, Blackburn. Part time work including kitchen and serving customers.

Referees:

Mr P Carter	Mrs T Nathubai
Carter & Son	Blackburn College
Leighton Drive	King William Street
Blackburn	Blackburn
(Manager)	(Course tutor)

The purpose of a cv is to give the reader the chance to see at a glance quite a lot about you in a number of ways:

1 *By what it actually says* – the qualifications you have and the work you have done.

2 *By the way it is presented* – a well presented cv tells the person reading it that you have taken some time and trouble over it and this suggests that you really want the job and that you are the sort of person who can make a good job of things.

3 *By what it does not say* – a firm may be looking for specific experience or qualifications and the cv lets them see at a glance if you have what they are looking for. If you do not have what they want this saves you coming for an interview and being disappointed when you do not get the job.

2 *Write a letter of application*

You looked at the right way to produce a letter in Unit 6 on business communications. An application letter should reveal clearly and concisely what makes you suitable for the job.

Using your knowledge of business communications, read the letter shown in Fig 15.2 and then rewrite it giving the same information but in a better way.

Direct Car Sales
24 Carshalton Square
Loughborough

Dear Sir
I am writing to apply for the job you put in the Gazette last Thursday for an office assistant. I am 17 years old and have just finished school.

I have worked in a few places while at school, and I have helped my dad in his business. The places I have worked are, McDonalds, Debenhams and the pizza bar on the square. I know a lot about working in offices from school and I've done some filing and typing in my part-time jobs. I've got a computer at home and I can type well.

I would like to work in your office because I want a job that lets me do different things and because it's close to where I live. I am very interested in cars and I am a very hard worker. You can check this with mr Halps at the pizza bar.

I hope I hear from you soon.
Yours

Nigel Thompson,

Fig 15.2

A good application letter will be:

- Clearly written or typed (good handwriting is better than poor typing)
- Polite and clear. It will explain some details about you, your experience and qualifications, why you think you could do the job and why you would like the job.
- To the point. Do not go into great detail about your hobbies or interests unless they are relevant to the job.
- Accompanied by a stamped addressed envelope.
- Written or typed on good, unlined paper, preferably fairly plain rather than a fancy colour or one with pictures on it.

3 Complete an application form

Application forms are designed by the firm for you to fill in with details about yourself. The form will probably ask for most of the information that you would put in a cv or in a letter of application. There are a few rules to follow when completing an application form:

- Write or type clearly. If you write the form use a black pen or ballpoint as this will photocopy more easily than other colours.
- If you can, photocopy the form and practise filling it in before you actually complete the one to send off so that you know how to space it neatly.
- Fill in all the questions. If a question does not apply to you write 'Not applicable'; if the answer is 'none', write this rather than leaving it blank.
- If there is information that you want to keep confidential put it on a separate sheet and seal it in an envelope marked 'For the attention of the personnel officer only' and attach it to the form when you send it in.

In whatever way you are asked to apply for a job remember that the forms or letters you send to them are the only way that the firm can judge whether to ask you for an interview. Remember the following points.

- Take your time. Do not rush.
- Plan what you want to say.
- Read the details about the job carefully and explain why you are suitable for it.
- Write or type clearly. If you write, use a dark colour.
- Answer all the questions you are asked.
- Tell the truth. Do not exaggerate or invent.
- Send the forms/letter in good time.
- Make sure you let them know where you can be contacted.
- Keep the details of the job so you can refresh your memory before the interview.
- Keep a copy of what you send to the firm so that you know what you have told them.

Interviews

When you are invited to attend an interview for a job this is your chance to impress the employer and prove you are the right person. It is also your chance to look at the firm and decide whether you would be happy there. Take full advantage of the chance to ask questions and look around – after all, if you get the job you will be spending a lot of time there. There are three stages to an interview:

1 Getting ready for the interview
2 Looking round the firm
3 The interview.

1 Getting ready for the interview

When you are asked to go for an interview the firm will probably ask you to let them know whether you will be attending or not. Do this as soon as you can – leaving it to the last minute leaves a bad impression.

You should have copies of the details of the job as well as the application that you sent and the firm may send you some more details with the invitation to interview. You will need to read all of this information before you go so that you know what to ask and what you have already mentioned in your application. If you can find out any more information about the firm that will be very useful as it will give you more to ask about and will also show that you are interested. There are a number of ways of finding out about a business:

- collect brochures on their products
- ask people who work there about the business
- contact their publicity department if they have one and explain that you have applied for a job with them and would like some more information about the firm.

Before you go for interview make two lists:

- *Questions I want to ask:* e.g. Could I get day release to go to college?
- *Questions they may want to ask me:* e.g. Have I any filing experience. *Answer:* Yes, at Johnsons and at Homecare.

Before the interview there are some things you should check:

- Do I know how to get there?
- How long will it take to get me there? If you are not sure of the route or the travelling time, check in advance and leave yourself plenty of time to get there. Do not cut your times down to the minute – if anything happens you could easily be late unless you have allowed some extra time.

- Where do I go and who do I ask for when I arrive? You may be told this on the details of the interview. If this information is not given telephone the firm and ask.
- Have I got suitable clothes for the interview? Are they clean? Do I need to have my hair done? Looking smart is important at an interview. The sort of clothes to wear will depend on the job that you have applied for but try to look smart and avoid 'high fashion' clothes. Make sure the clothes are clean and pressed.

2 Looking round the firm

Often, before the actual interview you will get a chance to look round the firm and to ask any questions that you want. This is your chance to find out some answers to the questions you have; it is also your chance to show them you are:

- keen
- aware of what the firm does
- pleasant and able to get on with people
- able to do the job
- willing to learn.

While you are being shown round you may get the chance to chat to people informally. If you do get the chance to do this try to find out as much as you can about the firm and the job to make sure that it is what you want and that you would be right for the job. Remember that very often the person who has shown you round or who you have chatted to over a coffee will be asked for their opinion of you. This is not 'snooping' – it is giving the people who you would be working with a chance to see what they think of the interviewees.

3 The interview

The actual interview can worry people a lot. You have got ten minutes, maybe half an hour, to convince a number of people you do not know that you are right for the job. You are nervous, not sure what they want and not sure what they think of you. That is natural. If you were not nervous it would probably mean that you were not that keen on the job anyway. The people who are interviewing you will know that you will be nervous and they will make allowances for it. What they want to know is:

- Can you do the job?
- Will you fit in?
- Are you the best person for the job?

So, how do you come across well?

- *Be yourself.* If you put on an act and pretend to be something you are not then they will probably be able to tell and, if you have to put on that much of an act to make it seem you are right for the job then you are probably not.
- *Be polite.* Greet the interviewers when you are shown in and thank them and say goodbye at the end of the interview.
- *Relax a bit.* Sit down when you are asked, without fidgeting, look at the interviewers and speak clearly. If you need a moment to think about a question, take it, a few seconds may seem a long time to be quiet but it is not noticeable to the interviewers.
- *Be honest.* Give honest answers to questions. If you have only had a little experience of some aspect of the job say that you only have a little experience and add that you would be keen to learn and are confident you could pick it up.
- *Ask what you want to know.* It is not cheeky to ask questions – it shows that you have thought about the firm and the job and that you are concerned to make sure that you are right for the job.

Most firms will try to let you know as soon as possible after the interviews whether you have got the job or not. If you are not told when you are likely to find out, then ask before you leave. You can then give them a ring if you have not had a letter within the time that they said.

Being offered a job

A job is an agreement between you and the person or firm you will work for. You agree to work for them. They agree to pay you. It is a little more complex than that but this is the basis of what is called the contract of employment. A contract is an agreement that you can go to court over if someone breaks it – so if your employer does not pay you you could go to court to get your money. Usually if someone is going to offer you a job they will send you a letter like the following one.

CHAPNOR SERVICES
2 High Street, Bradford BD1 1RL

Mr T Jackson
1 Compley Lane
Breightmet
BRADFORD BD4 3RQ

20 February 19--

Dear Mr Jackson

Thank you for coming to the interview last Thursday. We were very impressed with you and I would now like to offer you the job of section junior starting on the 14th of March.

We have already discussed the conditions of the job and I enclose some details with this letter. I would also like to invite you to come into the office for the day at 9.30 am on the 10th of this month to meet your section head, Peter Mann, and the rest of the section. We will pay you for the day and reimburse travelling expenses for you.

Please let me know, in writing, by the end of the week if you are prepared to accept the post and do not hesitate to contact me if you need any further details before the 10th.

Yours sincerely

G M Clark

G M Clark,
Personnel Manager

You should reply to a letter such as this one as soon as you can, whether you are taking the job or not. An example of a suitable reply is shown in Fig 15.3.

1 Compley Lane
Breightmel
BD4 3RQ

23 February 19--

Dear Mr Clarke

Thank you for your letter offering
me the job of section junior. I am
pleased to accept the job and
look forward to meeting you
again on the 10th.

Would it be possible for you to
send me some information on
the type of work that I will
be doing so that I can try to
familiarise myself with it before
I start?

Yours sincerely

T Jackson

T Jackson

Fig 15.3

Contract of employment

Once you have got a job you will get a **contract of employment**. This is a legal agreement between you and your employers which gives you some rights and responsibilities.

When you successfully get a job you have certain rights and responsibilities as an employee. To illustrate some of these read the story told by Carol:

'I applied for several jobs and eventually it was my lucky day. I went for an interview at . . . Oh, I had better not tell you the real name of the firm so I'll just call it Brax Ltd. I was really nervous at the interview. They told me all about the job and said I would be getting six weeks' holiday a year plus bank holidays. I was to be paid £90 per week. I couldn't believe it, it was my first real job – I was an office clerk.

'I started work in the office – most of the people seemed friendly. I enjoyed the job and worked really hard. Then one day I was told to clean the office because the cleaner was off ill. I wasn't very happy about this but did it. Several days later we were very quiet in the office and I was asked to go and wash the boss's car. I said no to this and my supervisor said that since we were quiet we had to do whatever other jobs we were asked to do. I still wouldn't clean the car so my supervisor just said: "Carol, I don't like cheek and disobedience, collect your things and go. We can do without people like you."

'I went to the job centre the next day to look for a new job. I got an interview for another office job but at the interview they asked me why I left my last job. I had to tell them I was sacked. "We'll let you know". But I didn't hear anything. I applied for several other jobs but the application forms all had a section for referees where I had to give the name and address of my previous employer . . .'

ACTIVITY

Carol's rights.

1 Do you think Carol should have been sacked for not washing the car?
2 Was Carol responsible for washing the car, cleaning the office and doing any other jobs during quiet times?
3 Why do you think Carol will find it difficult to get another job?

A contract of employment shows that the employee has agreed to do a certain job and the employer has agreed to pay a certain amount of wages or salary, to allow the employee to have a certain number of days holiday and so on. Because people often forget what is said at an interview an employee should be given a contract in writing or details of the contract within 13 weeks of starting work. The written details are normally called **written particulars**, the employer's name and address, job title, starting date, salary scale, intervals at which payment is made, working hours, holidays, sick pay entitlement, pension schemes, length of notice by both employer and employee, grievance procedures and any disciplinary rules applicable.

In Carol's case she had not been provided with a written statement and so Brax Ltd had broken the law.

The Employment Protection (Consolidation) Act 1978 states that within 13 weeks of starting work a full time employee must be given a written contract of employment or a statement of written particulars giving details of their employment.

It is quite in order to employ someone to be an office clerk and be a general helper as well, in which case some cleaning duties and possibly car cleaning would be acceptable. However, at Carol's interview there did not appear to be any mention of these general helper duties and of course it was not specified in her written contract as she was not given one.

The written statement sets out what you can be sacked on the spot for and what offences you will be given a warning for. Normally if you are late for work or your work is not up to the standard you may be given an oral warning. If there is no improvement you can be given a written warning and then a final written warning, after which you can be dismissed. For certain offences employers can dismiss employees instantly, e.g. being rude to customers and clients, theft, fighting or even smoking in a no smoking area. Whatever they are you should be told about them in your written statement.

Your rights and responsibilities

You have a number of rights at work and a number of responsibilities:

RIGHTS	RESPONSIBILITIES
Equal opportunities	Treat others fairly
Join a trade union	Do your job adequately
A safe place to work	Take care to work safely
Pay slip	Follow instructions
Notice if dismissed	Give notice if leaving
Not to be unfairly dismissed	Not to break your contract
A grievance procedure	

Your rights

Equal opportunities

It is against the law for an employer to treat you badly because

- you are disabled
- of your race, colour of skin or national origin
- you are female
- you are male.

You have to be given a fair chance to get a job, the same treatment as anyone else when you are in the job, proper access to promotion and training, and you cannot be picked on by being disciplined unfairly or selected for dismissal unfairly.

Read the case studies below and say whether you think the people concerned have been treated fairly.

1 Winston, who is black, applied for a job as a trainee chef. He had worked as a cook for a couple of years and had done a catering course at college. He did not get the job – it went to a white woman with no experience and no qualifications.

2 Alan applied for a job in an office doing the filing. It was essentially the same as the job he was doing but the money was better and he would be in charge of an assistant. The job went to a girl with no experience and Alan was told: 'The girls in the office don't want a man working there'.

3 Anoop, who is Asian, was made redundant from his job despite having been with the firm for a longer time than some of the people who kept their jobs.

4 Diana, a sales rep for three years, did not get promoted to sales manager on the grounds that 'The lads wouldn't take orders from you'. The man who got the job had only been a rep for a year.

The right to join a trade union

You have the right to join a trade union and you cannot be disciplined or dismissed for belonging to one.

The right to a safe place to work

It is the employer's responsibility to keep the workplace safe and there will often be safety representatives whose job it is to help to ensure that it is safe. If the employer does not keep the workplace safe he could be taken to court and fined, or even sent to prison.

The right to a pay slip

You have the right to get a payslip giving details of your pay and how it is worked out (*see* Fig 15.4). You should not be given a wage packet without these details or with just a total on it.

The right to notice

If you are dismissed from a job you have a right to a period of notice after you have been told that you are dismissed. The only time that this does not apply is if you have committed 'gross misconduct' – this means something so serious that the employer can order you off the premises at once and refuse to allow you back. Examples would include hitting someone at work or stealing from your employer.

```
+-------------------------------------------------------------------+
|                         PAY ADVICE                                |
+---------------------------------+---------------------------------+
| Name:                           | Works No:                       |
+-----------------+---------------+---------------------------------+
| Week No:        | Date:         | Code No:                        |
+-----------------+---------------+---------------------------------+
|                                                         £         |
|                                                                   |
| Earnings: basic pay                                               |
|           overtime                                                |
|           other                                        _____    |
|                                                                   |
| Total gross pay                                                   |
| Less pension                                           _____    |
| Gross pay for tax purposes                                        |
|                                                                   |
| Less deductions                          £                        |
|                                                                   |
|    Income tax                                                     |
|    National insurance                                             |
|    Savings                                                        |
|    Social fund                                                    |
|    Other                          _____                         |
|                                                                   |
| Total deductions                                       _____    |
|                                                                   |
| NET PAY                                                ========    |
+-------------------------------------------------------------------+
```

Fig 15.4 A pay advice slip

The right not to be unfairly dismissed

After you have worked in a place for two years you have the right not to be fired unless the employer has a good reason for doing so and has treated you fairly. If the employer does not dismiss you fairly you can go to an industrial tribunal (a sort of court) and be given compensation, or even get your job back. The employer can dismiss you for:

- gross misconduct
- repeated minor misconduct (lateness etc.)
- being unable to do your job
- constant illness and absence

and a few other reasons. However, they have to act fairly and they have to give you a statement of the reasons for dismissing you.

The right to a grievance procedure

If you feel that you are not being fairly treated by your employer you have the right to make your complaint through what is called a grievance procedure and to have it heard by someone unbiased.

Your responsibilities

Responsibility to treat others fairly

When you are at work you have to treat other people with consideration even if you do not agree with them or like them. You have already looked at this in the unit on business relationships (Unit 12).

Responsibility to do your job

Your contract with your employer is based on them paying you for doing a certain job. If you do not do the job or do it badly you will be in breach of your contract and may be subject to disciplinary procedures such as warnings.

Responsibility to work safely

Your employer has a duty to keep the workplace safe and you have the responsibility to avoid doing anything which might harm other people and to make sure that you follow safety rules and use safety equipment. If you do not follow safety rules, deliberately damage safety equipment or endanger people at work you might end up in court or even in prison.

Responsibility to follow instructions

When you take a job there is likely to be someone in charge of you. You have a responsibility to carry out your job in the way that they say and to follow reasonable instructions from them. They cannot ask you to do something which is dangerous to yourself or to other people and they cannot ask you to do something completely outside the job (such as in the example of Carol earlier in this unit).

Responsibility to give notice

If you are leaving a job you have to give your employers notice of the fact that you are leaving so that they can make arrangements to cover your work. Equally they have a duty to give you a period of notice if they dismiss you, although they may choose to pay you the notice and ask you not to come into work.

Summary

1 *People work for many reasons, for example, for money, to occupy themselves, to meet people, because they enjoy the job, and to gain experience.*

2 *Office work is done in many different kinds of organisations. The scope of office jobs will be different in different types of organisations.*

3 *Some of the ways you can find job vacancies are by looking in job centres, local newspapers, employment agencies, and noticeboards in the workplace. You can also write to firms directly and use personal contacts.*

4 *A Job Description tells you details of the job.*

5 *You may be asked to apply for a job by completing an application form, or writing a letter of application or sending a curriculum vitae or using a combination of these methods.*

6 *You are judged by the written information you send to firms when applying for a job. Make sure it is well written and presented and always keep a copy for your own reference.*

7 *Prepare for an interview by finding out about the organisation, considering the questions you may be asked, thinking of questions you may want to ask the interviewers, finding out how to get to the organisation and how long it takes.*

8 *At the interview be yourself, be polite, try to relax, be honest, and ask questions if you want to know information.*

9 *When an employer offers a job to an applicant, and the applicant accepts the job a legal contract is made.*

10 *Within 13 weeks of starting work, an employee should be given a written contract of employment or details of the contract in writing.*

11 *When you are at work you have certain rights and responsibilities.*

USING RESOURCES WITH CARE

16

This unit is designed to tell you:

- *What resources businesses have and use.*
- *Why resources have to be used carefully.*
- *How organisations keep track of resources and make sure they are used efficiently.*
- *What you can do to help use resources with care.*

When you have got a job and start working with an organisation you become part of the way the firm gets its work done – a resource. People are usually called **human resources**. People are one of the most important resources that a business can have – without good people to work for them businesses would not be able to operate at all.

Types of resource

The organisation uses resources to produce products or services for customers and clients. Its main resources are:

- people
- materials
- equipment and buildings
- services
- money.

A firm or organisation needs some or all of these resources in order to produce something or to carry out a service. Without the necessary resources the goods will not be produced or the jobs will not get done.

Read the descriptions of the two businesses below and try to decide what resources they are using. The first one has been started to help.

BUSINESS	RESOURCES
A window cleaning business going round a town and cleaning windows.	People to clean the windows Materials like soap Money to buy equipment and materials like soap Equipment such as . . . Services such as . . .
A corner newsagents selling some basic groceries and household goods as well as sweets, etc.	

Where do these resources come from?

Most firms start off with one resource, money, and use this to obtain the rest. Money for businesses can come from a number of sources:

- People setting up in business will use their savings and may use money that they can get from selling their houses or other property to help them to start in business.
- Banks will lend money to businesses provided they think that there is a good chance of getting the money back. This usually means that they will look at a business very carefully before putting money up for it.
- People can put money into a business by buying shares in it and getting some money back, known as a **dividend**, each year. If the company does well they will get a large dividend, if it does badly they may get none at all.
- Businesses make profits if they are successful and this money can be put back into the business to help it to grow and do even better in the future.

Once an organisation has money it can buy other resources that it needs. One thing to remember that it costs money to borrow money. Interest rates mean that you can pay quite heavily to borrow and the business has to make enough to pay the interest as well as paying for the original sum.

People

Businesses need people to do the work. Some businesses, known as **labour intensive businesses**, use a lot of people to get the work done. Other businesses, known as **capital intensive businesses**, use a lot of machines and equipment but very few people to get the work done.

ACTIVITY

Do you think these businesses are going to be capital intensive or labour intensive:

- a corner shop?
- a housebuilder?
- door to door cleaning materials selling?
- a computer shop?
- a disco?
- a car factory?
- a pub?

Small firms or businesses may only have a few people working for them; large businesses will have a lot of people doing all sorts of different jobs. People can be quite an expensive resource for a business. Look at the following example and work out how much they will spend on staff each year.

Gerry started his business selling cars about six years ago when he was made redundant from a garage and sold his house to raise some money. The business has grown now to the point where it is one of the biggest in the town. Gerry prides himself on his work and reckons that this is why he has done well – he gives a good service and people come back and they tell their friends. He started with just himself and a salesman. They are now the manager and deputy manager and each make £20 000 per year. After two years they took on another salesman and they have now got two, making about £10 000 per year each. So as to have control over the work on cars he bought a small garage last year and employs a mechanic and assistant – they cost him £17 000 per year between them in wages. To keep the office work under control they have got two people who come in part time and make £3000 per year each. There is a cleaner to pay who keeps the showroom and offices clean, that is about £2000 a year, and Gerry pays about £1000 a year for car cleaning – mostly schoolkids at weekends and after school.

Materials

Most businesses need materials of some sort in order to get the work done, in an office you might use

- power to light and heat the office
- paper
- stationery supplies like paperclips and pens
- computer disks
- printer ribbons

and a lot of other things. While some of these items are cheap on their own they add up across the year to a great deal of money. If you have 30 typewriters using one ribbon every three weeks, and the ribbons cost £6.50 each, you could spend nearly £3400 on typewriter ribbons alone. Some businesses have to work with very expensive materials, like jewellers who need to buy gold and precious stones or computer firms that have to buy expensive components.

It is important to keep track of all the materials to make sure that they do not get damaged accidentally or stolen and that the business does not run out of the materials needed to do the job. You looked at the way some materials are controlled in Unit 9 on stock handling. Nowadays a lot of businesses keep account of their stock of materials using computer systems which can tell them exactly how much they have left. You can see sophisticated systems in many supermarkets where the tills which scan goods are linked to a computer, telling the manager:

- exactly how many items, tins of baked beans say, they have left in the shop
- which items are selling best
- which items they need to reorder
- which items are out of stock
- what is not selling well
- the total value of the stock in the shop.

In one supermarket recently the manager found that they had £4 500 000 of stock on the premises at the start of the weekend rush.

ACTIVITY

In order to be effective an office has a lot of functions – one of the main jobs of an office is to help keep track of the paperwork. Make a list of the materials that you think an office needs to do the paperwork for a business. Do not forget things like power, tea and coffee, lightbulbs, paper for typing and computers.

Equipment and buildings

Equipment and buildings can be very expensive resources for a business to buy. They are rather different from the materials that the business uses up as they will last for quite a long time. Even computers, which get out of date very quickly, can give five years' work or more. Some businesses need a lot of equipment and buildings to get the work done and do not need many people. In Japan some companies have built 'people-less' factories which only have a few people to operate the machines and keep them running or repair them if they break down.

Other businesses need a lot of people to do the work, but not much in the way of equipment or buildings. Because they are so expensive to buy, quite a lot of companies and businesses rent or 'lease' buildings and equipment. This means that they do not have to find all the money for the purchase at once. They pay for the machine or the building every year rather than paying for it once. Leasing is frequently used for machines which have to be replaced quite often like computers, photocopiers or company cars because it means that the business does not have the problem of getting rid of the old machine when it wants a new one – that is the leasing company's problem.

ACTIVITY

What sort of equipment might a modern office have to have, e.g. desks, computers and photocopiers?

Services

Most businesses need to have some services provided in order for them to be able to work. This will include:

- professional services like solicitors and accountants
- cleaning services
- maintenance of machines and equipment.

Large companies may have their own people to do all these jobs – technicians, cleaners, mechanics, solicitors – all working full time for the business. Smaller organisations may not have enough work to keep someone in one of these jobs busy all the time and they have to choose between paying for someone to work for them part time or calling in firms from outside to do the jobs for them when they are needed.

Why use resources with care?

One of the responsibilities that you have at work is to do your job well in order to help the business or organisation achieve its targets. These vary as the following list indicates:

- Many are trying to make as much money as they can so that they can grow, keep on providing jobs and paying people.
- Some, like charities, are concerned to keep their costs as low as possible so that the money they get in can go to the people who need it.

- Government and local authority organisations are usually trying to provide a service to the public and have to make sure that they do not waste any of the money provided.

What they all have in common is that they can achieve their goals better if they keep their costs as low as possible. One of the best ways to do that is to use all the resources of the business with care. This is *everyone's* responsibility – not just the managers or bosses.

ACTIVITY

Read the study below and make a note of where you think resources are being wasted.

'Morning Tom,' said Anita as she came into the office, 'cold today isn't it?' 'Is it?' replied Tom, 'I'll close the window then.' 'No, it's all right, I know you like the fresh air, I'll put the fan heater on.' Later that morning Sharon came into the office looking for a ribbon for the computer from the stock cupboard. Tom, grumbling, gave her one; 'What do you do to these Sharon? You got three last week.' 'I know, I put them on the window sill and forgot them and they've dried up.' In the afternoon the photocopy engineer called to service the copier and complained that it was low on toner. 'That'll be Tom' volunteered Sharon, getting her own back, 'he always forgets which way to put the copies in and comes back to find he's got 30 copies of half a page. Then he has to do them again.'

About four o'clock the office was nearly empty and Tanya from Accounts came in – not seeing anyone in the room she switched the lights off. 'Hey!' called Anita 'leave those on, I can't see a thing.' 'Sorry, Anita', I didn't see you – but why do you have to have the whole floor lit up when there's only you here?'

Businesses can save money by being careful about how they use resources – that is why there are so many signs in offices and businesses reminding you to switch lights off and to close windows to stop heat getting out in the winter. In a recent economy drive in one government department they reported a saving of £150 000 worth of electricity in one year.

What can you do to keep costs down?

- Always remember to switch lights and machines off if they are not needed.
- Try to use the phone at cheap times rather than at peak times – or could you send a letter instead of a long distance call?
- Choose the best way of copying documents – the photocopier is best for small numbers but you may be able to send large amounts off for printing.
- Report any minor faults or hazards as soon as you can – if they are dealt with early they will probably cost less to fix.

- Plan phone calls before you make them and have all the information you need to hand.
- Make sure you follow instructions on machines so as not to damage them or get things wrong.
- Try not to waste paper, paperclips and similar small items – they all mount up as costs.
- If you have any suggestions as to how the firm could save money tell your manager or supervisor, or if there is a suggestion scheme put forward your ideas.
- Use the most economical way to send letters and parcels – there's no need for everything to go first class.
- Do not use the fax if a letter or phone call will do instead.

Summary

1 *An organisation's resources are people, materials, equipment and buildings, services and money.*

2 *Resources are expensive and need to be used with care.*

3 *Always consider cost when doing tasks such as copying documents, using the telephone and sending letters and parcels.*

4 *Small items cost money too and should not be wasted because the cost can mount up.*

FITTING INTO YOUR ORGANISATION

17

This unit is designed to tell you about:

- *The different sorts of organisation.*
- *How they are organised.*
- *What the main departments do.*
- *What goals organisations have.*
- *How you go about fitting into your organisation.*

Organisations

There are many types of organisation such as shops, accountants, solicitors, dry cleaners, bus companies, hospitals and schools. These organisations are all different but they all have some things in common:

- they are organised and keep records
- they are owned
- they have goals to achieve
- they provide services and/or products to customers/clients
- they use resources
- they change to meet changing needs.

Being organised

Organisations need to be 'organised' so that they can provide a reliable and efficient service to their customers and clients. In order to provide a service goods need to be bought and paid for, products made and sold and records kept. The public need to know about the service. Stock needs to be kept and deliveries made. These jobs need to be organised in some way to ensure they are done quickly, efficiently and correctly.

In small organisations many jobs are carried out by one person but in large organisations there are specialist people employed to do different types of job. A large organisation is divided into departments to make it easier to manage. For example the departments may include:

1 *Stores* – stores and keeps records of raw materials and finished products.
2 *Purchasing* – finds suppliers and orders goods.

3 *Sales* – finds customers and arranges sales.

4 *Marketing* – researches the needs of customers and lets the public know that the organisation exists.

5 *Accounts* – keeps records of costs, sales and profits and plans the money side of the business.

6 *Personnel* – finds and trains staff and deals with the people side of the organisation.

7 *Wages* – calculates and pays wages.

8 *Delivery* – delivers goods to customers.

9 *Production* – manufactures products.

10 *Office services* – deals with mail, switchboard, filing, reception, typing and data processing.

Each of these departments will have office work where data processing is done, letters and memos prepared, mail dealt with, telephone calls made, enquiries dealt with, filing done and records kept.

Organisation charts

As organisations are complex you will often come across organisation charts which try to explain who is who and show what departments there are in the organisation.

All organisations are different due to their size, the way they have grown in the past, their departments, and the services they offer or type of products they produce. This means that they have different structures, which can be shown on a special chart, known as an organisation chart. It shows who is responsible to whom and for what.

Here are some examples of organisation charts. Each chart tells a story about the firm which it represents.

Fashion Fads: a fashion boutique

Fashion Fads is a small organisation. The manager is Anne Jackson, who is also the owner of the firm. She has four part-time members of staff working for her – three part-time sales staff and one part-time clerk.

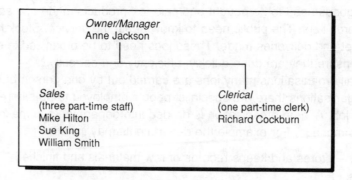

Owner/Manager
Anne Jackson

Sales
(three part-time staff)
Mike Hilton
Sue King
William Smith

Clerical
(one part-time clerk)
Richard Cockburn

Fig 17.1 Organisation chart of Fashion Fads

Make a list of jobs which you think are done by:

1 The owner/manager
2 Sales staff
3 The clerk.

Wilkinson Ltd

Wilkinson Ltd is a fairly large organisation. The managing director is Mr
Wilkinson and he has responsibility for six managers each responsible for
a different aspect of the business. Each of the managers has responsibility
for certain areas. For example, Mr Maken is the production manager and
he is responsible for the quality control and production team. Mr Bryan is
the personnel manager with responsibility for training, recruiting staff and
safety.

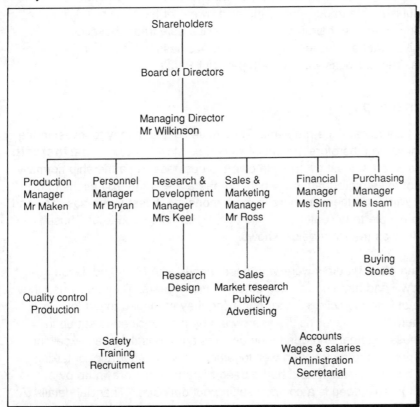

Fig 17.2   Organisation chart of Wilkinson Limited

Finish the story, stating which manager is in charge of each area of the business
and what each is responsible for.

Who owns organisations?

Organisations do not just exist. They are created by someone or by several people. As organisations get bigger they tend to have more owners.

Sole traders

If an organisation has only one person as the owner it is called a **sole trader**. The sole trader provides the money for the business and keeps the profit.

As an example, Paul trained as a hairdresser at his local college. When he qualified he set up as a mobile hairdresser going round hospitals, homes for the elderly, private houses and hotels. As he built more trade he employed another hairdresser to work for him on a full-time basis.

Paul is a sole trader – he is the sole owner of the business. When he employed another hairdresser he was still a sole trader because he did not give that hairdresser any part of the business but paid her a weekly wage. The business was still 100 per cent Paul's.

Partnerships

Sole traders can face problems. They have limited money to invest in the business and therefore the business can be slow to grow. A **partnership** exists when at least two people own the business. A partnership normally cannot have more than 20 owners but there are some exceptions to this rule. With a partnership there is more money to invest in the business and more people to look after and manage it. Partners need to be chosen carefully as the story below shows.

Jill and Mark Webrow were very good friends with Mary and Jason Chadwill and had known each other for many years. They met when they were at catering college. After qualifying they managed to get jobs in restaurants. However as the years went by they decided to set up in business together and open their own restaurant as they had excellent experience and they got on well together – and so after a lot of talking they became partners and had a deed of partnership drawn up by a solicitor. This deed is a contract setting out duties and financial details. At first the partnership worked well but two years later they had terrible rows and their friendship deteriorated. They accused each other of all sorts of things and eventually sold the business at a loss, just to get out.

Partnerships can have many problems especially those concerned with working relationships. Knowing people as friends socially is different from working with them.

Private limited companies

Sole traders and partners in a partnership own and manage their business. They have the profits if the business does well – a sole trader has all the profits to him/herself, and partners share the profits. But if the business makes a loss, the sole trader or partnership has to pay the business' debts out of their own pocket. For this reason some businesses are set up as **private limited companies**.

Private limited companies have a minimum of two people owning the business. The owners are called **shareholders** although they do not necessarily manage the business themselves. It is managed by a board of directors and it is usual for some of the shareholders to manage the business by being members of the board of directors. Private limited companies can be large organisations but many are very small indeed with only a few shareholders.

The advantage of an organisation being a private limited company is that if the company makes a profit the shareholders have some of the profit or dividend but if the business gets into financial difficulty the shareholders are not liable to pay the firm's debts.

Public limited companies

Public limited companies are massive organisations. They raise money through selling shares to the public at large. Private limited companies cannot do this and, therefore, the shareholders in a private company are normally family and friends.

Private and public sector organisations

Sole traders, partnerships and private limited companies are all **private sector organisations** which means that they are owned by one or more people rather than being owned and run by the government. Most businesses that you deal with and buy goods from are owned by individuals who want to make a profit from them. The larger businesses, like department stores, are probably public limited companies; others will be private limited companies, partnerships or sole traders. Sole trader businesses are often small, like market stalls, small cafés or shops. If you take a walk around the centre of your town you will see all different sizes of private sector businesses operating.

Some organisations are said to be 'in the public sector'. They are held by the government in trust for the people of the country. So you could say that they are government-owned or that they are owned by everyone. Public sector organisations provide a lot of the services we use everyday such as street lights, pavements, schools and hospitals. They may be run locally by the council in the case of services like refuse collection and street repairs; or they may be run by central government in the case of things like building new motorways, providing unemployment benefit and collecting taxes. Most public sector organisations do not sell goods – they provide services instead so their customers are the people to whom they provide a service.

Whether a business is in the private or public sector it will still need people to work in it and make sure it runs properly. In a public sector organisation you will probably be part of a large department and have a very clear job. In a private sector organisation, especially if it is a small one, you may have many different jobs to do.

The organisation's goals

All organisations have goals. The goals may be to achieve a certain amount of profit, to grow bigger, or even to stay in business. In order to achieve them people or sections within the organisation are normally given targets to meet. For example:

- Sales – to make a certain number of sales per week.
- Marketing – to attract a certain number of new customers.
- Production – to make a certain number of products.

If the organisation does not achieve its goals it may eventually face closure. All employees in the organisation have to work together and meet their targets to achieve success – it takes team effort.

Quite often there are goals or targets set from each of the sections in the business and these will have to be met by the people in the team or section. Targets for an office could include:

- to process a certain number of invoices per hour
- to input a certain amount of data per hour
- to make up a certain amount of wage packets before 11.30 am
- to answer customer queries within two days of them arriving
- to reduce the number of errors in invoices.

In order to help the business to achieve its overall goals you need to help your section meet its own targets and, to do this you need to fit into the organisation and be an effective member of the team that you work with.

How do you go about fitting in?

There are a number of key factors to help you fit into the organisation:

1 *Get to know what the organisation does, what it wants to achieve and who is who.* In a small business or organisation you can get to know people and what they do very quickly and they will probably talk about what they want for the organisation: 'We want to open a new branch next year' or 'We're going to be moving to bigger premises if sales are as good

as this for the rest of the year'. In a bigger organisation it can be harder as there are more people and there is therefore more to find out. You can probably get some information from your manager or supervisor and they may be able to tell you about the goals of the organisation: 'This company aims to be the biggest supplier in the country in three years' or 'There's a target of another 25 branches to be opened next year'.

The advantages of getting to know your organisation and what it aims to do are that you can get information more quickly and have greater job satisfaction and involvement. You will gain a wider understanding of what is happening. Questions such as: 'Will we be getting the invoices to do for the new branch next month?' or 'Are we getting these orders through faster because of the new computer system in accounts?' show that you know what your business is trying to achieve.

2 *Do your job well* – try to meet the targets that are set for you or your section. Doing your job well means that you can take pride in what you do and so the business will have less errors to correct and more time and resources to devote to getting on with the goals. Apart from helping the organisation, if you work hard you could be lining yourself up for a promotion to a better job, more pay or a bonus of some sort. Sometimes it is easy to think that no one notices what you do, and that they will not see if you do not bother about what you do – but they will. They may not say anything but people notice good workers; and it is the people who work well who get on in their jobs or get good references to go to another job with.

3 *Help other people when you can* – if you do they will help you in the future when you need it. Your time at work will be more pleasant if you get on with people you work with, and one way is to be helpful. Also, if you get on well with the people at work you will probably find that the work gets done faster, that there are fewer mistakes made and that you enjoy your work a lot more. Getting on with people takes some effort on both sides – but it never hurts to make the first move.

4 *Stick to the way that the company likes to work* – you do not have to become a company clone but you do have to stick to their rules and their way of doing things so that the business gives the impression that they want it to give. If they have rules on dress, on the way that documents are laid out or on the way that you answer the phone and deal with customers, they are there for a reason and you should keep to them.

5 *Be flexible where you can* – try to pick up new skills and new ways of working. Your contract probably states that you have to do 'other duties as may reasonably be required from time to time', or something like that. You do not have to do whatever you are asked and, if you are treated unreasonably you can use the grievance procedure to argue your point but try to be as flexible about your job as you can. Also, if you are flexible about the way that you do your job and are willing to help where you can this may mean that the firm is prepared to be flexible with you if you need it.

Summary

1 *All organisations have goals. These goals may be related to making profit, achieving growth and/or staying in business.*

2 *Targets are set for people or sections within organisations to enable the organisation's goals to be achieved.*

3 *To help you to fit into the organisation you should get to know what the organisation does and who is who, do your job well, help other people when you can, follow the rules, and be flexible by learning new skills.*

4 *There are many different types and sizes of organisations.*

5 *Large organisations have many departments such as stores, purchasing, sales, marketing, accounts, personnel, wages, production, office services etc.*

6 *The structure of an organisation is shown by an organisation chart.*

7 *The following organisations are in the private sector: sole trader, partnership, private limited companies, public limited companies.*

8 *Public sector organisations are owned by everyone.*

MAKING YOUR ORGANISATION LOOK GOOD

18

This unit is designed to tell you about:

- *What is meant by the image of an organisation.*
- *How organisations put across a particular image.*
- *How you help to put across the image of your organisation.*
- *How things change and the business keeps up to date.*

The image of the organisation

Rolls Royce, Jaguar, Jaeger – what do they have in common? One thing that they have in common is that they are all seen as 'high quality' firms making products of a good quality and charging a high price for them. This is known as their **image** – the way we see them. Every organisation has an image although it may not be as well known as the ones just mentioned. Some organisations have good images, others not so good – they may be seen as producing shoddy goods, as not being reliable or not providing an efficient service. Most large organisations try very hard to give themselves a good image as do a lot of smaller organisations.

ACTIVITY

Choose the words that you think fit the image of the firms listed below. You can add other words as well if you want to:

Cheap	Fashionable	Poor service	Solid
Value for money	Good service	Scruffy	Pushy
Poor quality goods	Expensive	Quality goods	Messy
Nice to deal with	Shoddy	Friendly	

BUSINESS	IMAGE
Marks and Spencer	
Dixons	
McDonalds	
Topshop	
Next	
Rover	
BMW	
Kentucky Fried Chicken	

How do firms go about creating an image?

- advertising
- public relations
- service
- correspondence
- premises.

All of these and more go into making up the image of an organisation.

Advertising

Advertising is one of the most important ways of creating an image, especially for a large organisation that can afford adverts on the TV and radio, posters and pages in the press. Small organisations also use advertising but they spend less – this may mean that they take smaller adverts across the whole country, or, as with a lot of local businesses, they advertise locally rather than across the whole country. Adverts give an organisation a chance to show people how they want to be seen and some of them are very effective.

ACTIVITY

Look at the adverts in your local papers, in magazines and on TV. Choose three that you think are trying to put across a particular image and make a note of the image you think they want you to have. Try to choose ones that are putting across different images.

ADVERT	IMAGE

Advertising depends in part on market research done by the organisation to find out what people think about it, where they get their customers from and what they should do to promote the organisation. A large organisation may have its own special sections or firms employed to do this. In a smaller business there may only be some simple research like asking customers 'Where did you find out about us?' Whatever the size of the organisation everyone can help with market research by keeping their eyes and ears open, listening to what people say about the business and reporting the information back to their managers.

Public relations

Public relations is a bit like advertising. This is the phrase used to describe the way that some firms get their names in front of the public and associate them with a particular image. For example a lot of sports manufacturers will pay athletes and sports people to wear their goods. Insurance and financial companies will sponsor events that they think will fit in with their image so that their name gets in front of the right people. On a smaller scale a local firm may have an open day for customers or may have a special event like when a car dealer has a new model to launch, invites people to go to the garage for an evening to see the new car and provides some refreshments for people.

House style

Many organisations have their own **house style** – their way of doing things. This can include:

1 *The way employees dress* – the employer may provide a uniform or merely insist on a certain style of clothes. Whichever they do they are trying to make sure that the people who work for them will give customers the right image.
2 *The way letters and other material going out of the organisation are produced*. Insisting on a particular standard means that the employer can be sure that a customer will always get the same impression of the organisation, i.e. no one should get handwritten notes, all letters have to be typed on headed paper and so on.
3 *The way customers are treated*. If you walk into one branch of the business you will be treated in exactly the same way, or as close to it as possible, as you would be at all the other branches.
4 *The way phone calls are answered*. 'Yeah. Can I help you?' does not sound as professional as 'Good morning, Slater Howarth and Partners. How may I help you?' If people know what is expected they will be able to stick to it.
5 *The way the premises are decorated*. If you walk into a branch of, say, McDonalds, it will be very similar to most of the other branches that you have ever been into – the same image right across the organisation.

ACTIVITY

Select two organisations, one large and one small, and say what image you think they have. Once you have done that try to think how you have got that image and make a note of it. An example has been filled in to give you the idea.

FIRM	IMAGE	WHY
Volvo	Safe, quality, pricey	Adverts stress safety Look good Nice premises

Helping to keep your organisation looking good

What can you do to keep the organisation looking good?

- Keep to the rules concerning clothes, answering the phone, dealing with customers and sending out correspondence so that the image of the organisation is maintained.
- Think about the image of the organisation when you are talking to customers and make what you say fits in with it.
- Make sure that you meet the standards of customer service that the organisation wants – a satisfied customer is your best advert.
- Make a note of anything that does not fit in with the image and mention it to your manager or supervisor.

Keeping the image up to date

We live in a rapidly changing world and organisations have to change if they want to stay looking good. What was good business this year may not be so good next year and ideas need continually updating, e.g. many firms are now trying to present an environment-friendly or 'green' image.

What sort of changes are there?

1 *Competition:* organisations have competitors who bring in new products, lower prices or better quality products. If this happens the organisation will have to change their products or prices to keep ahead of, or at least not fall behind, its competitors. Organisations can also suffer from an out-of-date image – if your competitor has better advertising than you and the public starts to see them as being better than you, you will lose customers even if their products are no better than yours.

2 *Customers and fashions:* customers' tastes change, their habits change and their lifestyles change. This means that the products and services they want to purchase also change. In order to cope with this firms use market research to find out what their customers want and then they try to provide it. The problem with this is that it is easy to make a mistake and produce something that no one really wants whereas a new product, or one that looks different (e.g. round tea bags), may corner the market. Firms may also have a problem changing fast enough to meet the changing needs of customers if fashions move very fast.

3 *Equipment:* new equipment comes onto the market to make production easier or the flow of information faster. It changes the nature of some jobs. When computers were introduced they replaced lots of jobs in offices and they produced new work for input clerks, programmers and computer technicians. Firms need to be able to take advantage of any equipment that will enable them to do their job faster, cheaper or better, and that means having flexible staff who can pick up new ways of working and new skills when they need to.

Pick a firm or organisation you know well and say how and why it has changed in the last few years.

Summary

1 *The image of an organisation is the way it is seen by the public.*

2 *Most organisations try to present a good image.*

3 *Organisations create an image in many ways, for example, by advertising and public relations activities, by the services they provide, by the correspondence they send out, and by their premises.*

4 *You can help to keep up your organisation's image by keeping rules concerning dress, and when dealing with customers and clients.*

5 *Keeping customers satisfied gives your organisation a good image.*

6 *Organisations are affected by change. They need to respond to change to keep ahead of the market.*

KEEPING YOUR CUSTOMERS SATISFIED

19

This unit is designed to:

- *Explain the importance of keeping customers happy.*
- *Look at how best to keep customers satisfied.*
- *Suggest ways of handling problems with customers.*

This unit draws on a lot of what you have looked at in the rest of the book. In Unit 18 you looked at how an organisation puts across an image of itself to attract customers. Once an organisation has successfully given people an image they will expect it to actually be what it has suggested it is. If you have spent a lot of time and trouble putting across an image of good service do not be surprised if customers complain loudly about any poor service they get from you – they are not interested in your problems, you said you provided good service, so where is it?

Most customers will want:

- what you are selling or doing to meet the standard that they expect
- the way you serve them and treat them to fit the image that the organisation puts across.

How to satisfy customers?

By knowing who your customers are

If you work in a shop it is fairly obvious who your customers are – the people who come in and buy goods. It is less clear if you work in, say, a job centre – are your customers the people who come in looking for help with finding a job, the people who place adverts looking for people to work for them, or other people at work who depend on the information that you pass on to them so that they can do their jobs? Pick the answer you think is right:

- the people looking for jobs
- the people looking for staff
- the people wanting information
- all of them.

Right, all of them. They are all your customers and you need to try to keep all of them satisfied.

Spot the customer. Alan works in the finance office of a large firm. His job involves working out some of the wages and passing this information on to the accounts section who need it to produce the month end figures. He is also responsible for checking the wages of the people in one of the sections in the organisation and answering any queries they may have. Who are his customers?

By knowing what your customers expect

In order to know what your customers expect you need to know what sort of image they have of you. It is useful to know a bit about the organisation and to take an interest in the way that it works – that way you will have a good idea what people inside and outside the organisation think of it and, within the firm, what people think of your section.

Knowing your products/services

It makes no difference if you are selling cars, answering questions about wages or processing invoices – if you know what you are dealing with you will be able to answer questions easily and provide people with the information they need to help them.

By doing your job well

If everyone does their job well there will be very few problems. This should mean that goods always go out on time to the right place. Nothing ever gets lost. People are always delighted with the service they get. Unfortunately life is not like that. You will make mistakes and so will other people but you should try to make sure there are as few as possible.

By being pleasant and making an effort to get on with people

Being nice to people is one of the most effective ways of making them happy with you and the organisation. How many times have you heard people say that a firm is unpleasant? What they really mean is that someone who works for the firm was unpleasant to them. Even if someone starts off unpleasant to you it is best to try to be polite, and if that has no effect, do not get angry back – go and get someone else to try and deal with the customer.

Dealing with problems

'You can't please all of the people all of the time'. This is true, and if you deal with customers a lot you may feel that you get more than your fair share of the ones who are dissatisfied. In dealing with problems and complaints you have to be especially careful as to what you say and what you do. A customer who comes back to complain about something or who rings up to talk about a problem has already had their image of your organisation damaged. The organisation has invested a lot of time and money giving a high quality image and now something has gone wrong. If you are dealing with the person it is up to you to try and repair the damage. This applies as much if you are dealing with a shopper who has returned poor goods or if you are dealing with someone who has phoned up to complain that their wage slip is wrong. In either case you do not want their image of the organisation to be worse after dealing with you:

- 'What a firm – sell you shoddy stuff and try to make you feel it's your fault when you complain.'
- 'That's typical of that lot in the office – foul things up and then get nasty when you try to sort it out.'

If you handle a complaint properly you can go a long way to repairing the damage that it has done.

Remember the following points.

1 Quite often a customer with a genuine complaint has the law on their side. If someone is sold poor goods, or you describe something wrongly to them they can take you to court if you do not refund their money or replace the goods for them. It is usually better to deal with something before the customer is angry enough to go to court or to the local Trading Standards Department. If you feel that they do not really have a valid complaint but they will not accept this, then pass them on to your supervisor or manager to deal with.

2 Stay polite. When someone comes to complain they are probably nervous and wound up; so it is only natural that they may be a bit sharp at first. Most people, if you stay polite and calm will act the same way – after all they will probably realise that it is not your fault and, if you are doing your best to deal with it for them, they will be quite easy to deal with.

3 Where someone has a genuine complaint, apologise. Many organisations never think of saying sorry if there has been a problem but it will usually help to calm people down and restore the image of the organisation that you want. If someone has to wait for a long time to see about their complaint, for example, you could perhaps offer them a coffee.

Summary

1 Customers have certain expectations about your products and/or service.

2 To keep your customers satisfied you need to know your customers and their expectations. You need to know about your products and services and you need to be able to do your job well and be pleasant to people.

3 When a customer complains, the damage done to the organisation's image needs to be repaired by handling the complaint properly.

4 When customers complain, be polite and apologise. If the complaint is genuine the customer is likely to have the law on their side.

5 Many organisations have set procedures for dealing with complaints and you should follow these at all times. If you cannot deal with a complaint pass it on to your supervisor.

ASSIGNMENTS AND ACTIVITIES

20

This unit is designed to:

- *Provide you with practice and help for the work role competences.*
- *Give you a further chance to practise some of the clerical tasks.*

ASSIGNMENT 1

Suggestion box

Money can always be saved through using resources more efficiently. Read the suggestions which staff from Ainscough Insurance Services put forward to help use resources more efficiently.

A bright idea

It was noticed that when doing computer printouts there was substantial wastage of paper because the computer printed out several blank sheets at the beginning and end of each run.

The following suggestions were put forward to help put this blank paper to some use rather than putting it in the waste bin.

1 Collect the paper for recycling.
2 Make the paper into scrap pads.
3 Overprint and make the paper into message pads.
4 Donate it to the local nursery school as a public relations exercise.

YOUR TASK

Think of a bright idea to help use resources more efficiently in your workplace. Your idea could be labour saving, energy saving, time saving, cost saving, materials saving or could be a combination.

Here's how

1 Watch and question why things are done the way they are.
2 Identify inefficiencies.
3 Have a bright idea to increase efficiency.
4 Prepare a written report for the suggestion box using a word processor or typewriter. Your report should include the following points:

- the existing methods of working.
- your suggestion.
- the advantages of your suggestion in terms of savings, e.g. time saving, labour saving, whatever is relevant.

ASSIGNMENT 2

Special offer

You work as a cashier in Kylde Service Station. The parent company is keen to promote its own brand of oil, X8000.

X8000 is a top quality oil but is highly priced. To encourage customers to buy X8000, promotional gifts are offered free with the purchase of a five-litre can – this month the free gift is a blank audio cassette. The cashier also has the option of offering £1 discount instead of the free gift, or alternatively can allow the customer a free oil change.

The target for the service station is to sell 18 litres of oil per thousand gallons of petrol. Approximately one thousand gallons of petrol are sold per eight hour shift so you need to sell 18 litres of oil per day.

The company maintains that if the cashier does the job properly and points out the offer to the customers the target is achievable. Bonus incentives are given at the end of the month if the targets are achieved. The bonus is 10p per litre.

Draw up a sales strategy on how you plan to sell X8000 oil and achieve your target.

YOUR TASK

Information

PRICES OF OIL		
Brand	**Price per litre**	**Price per five litres**
X8000	£2.49	£9.99
PAE25		£4.99

Selling techniques
1 Point out monetary advantages of buying five litres of X8000.
2 Draw attention to the special offer.
3 Point out that the customer would need to change oil at some time and, therefore, may as well buy while there is a special offer.

4 Have a point of sale oil display.

5 If a customer goes to buy a blank audio tape inform the customer that there is a free cassette tape with X8000.

6 Point out the advantages of X8000 to the customer and sell the benefits.

7 Tell the customer the advantages and benefits of X8000 over PAE25.

8 Know your product knowledge well – there needs to be quick service in a service station and, therefore, you need to respond to customers' questions immediately.

Customer buying habits

1 When customers choose oil they tend to choose the cheapest. To meet your target of 18 litres of X8000 you need to bring the brand to the attention of the customer.

2 Customers do not like buying oil but there are obviously advantages of buying a good oil which customers may not know about. Product knowledge is, therefore, important.

X8000 PRODUCT KNOWLEDGE	
Advantages	**Benefits**
Multigrade oil	Suits all cars
Resists high temperatures	Suitable for turbo and performance cars
Has synthetic additives to prevent decay	Protects better and longer
Special pouring spout	Keeps engine clean

ASSIGNMENT 3

Creating an image

Every organisation has an image – that is the way it is viewed by the public, especially customers and clients. Organisations can work hard at creating an image through, for example, advertising and training. However, some of the money spent on creating an image is wasted if employees do not help to promote the image.

1 **Find out what image your firm is trying to promote. Ask your manager, use your experience and observation, look at the organisation's adverts, etc. Can you sum up the image of your organisation in a few words or lines?**

2 **Find out how this image is promoted. Make a note of answers to the following questions.**

- **How does the organisation promote its products or services?**
- **Where does the organisation advertise and how?**
- **Does training help to promote the image?**
- **Do staff wear uniforms?**
- **Is there a house style for letters and phone calls, etc?**

3 **Analyse whether reality matches up. Look through the eyes of a customer and:**

- **Go outside the building where you work and walk in again. What impression or image is given by the building?**
- **Walk past the reception and any public areas. What impression or image is given by the reception area, the reception staff and any other public areas? Is it well signed?**
- **Listen to staff answering the telephone and dealing with the public. What impression is given?**
- **Does reality match up to the image the organisation is trying to promote? If not, what improvements can be made?**

Make a note of the ways you think the organisation meets the image and where you think there are problems. Many of these things you can do nothing about, but where you can – like the way you answer the phone – make a note of how to improve. If your organisation has a suggestion scheme maybe you could put in some ideas.

4 **Identify ways in which you can help to promote the right image. Think of your job and what image you create. Can you help to give a good image? Make a list of the ways that you can help to give a good image. An example is given.**

WHAT CAN I DO . . .	HOW CAN I DO IT . . .
Answering the phone	Being polite and friendly
	Taking a message accurately

ASSIGNMENT 4

Where do you fit?

An assignment to do at work.

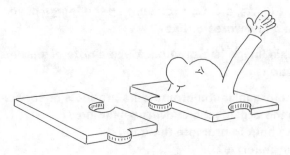

An organisation can only meet its aims if employees do their job conscienciously and well. Like a jigsaw puzzle where every piece is needed to make a complete picture, jobs within organisations fit together too. This makes employees depend on each other – it is called team work!

1 **Find out how your organisation works:**

- **Are there departments? What are they? What do they do? Make up a table to show the departments or sections and what they do.**
- **Draw or obtain an organisation chart. If one does not already exist you will need to produce it clearly and neatly. If there is one already make sure that it has enough detail on it – if not you may have to make a few additions.**

2 **Explain where you fit in**

- **What is your job? Make a note of your: job title, department or section, and main tasks (you may need to look at your job description).**
- **Who depends on you doing your job well? What information/work do they need?**

3 **Explain the consequences to your customers and fellow employees if you:**

- **are absent from work?**
- **are late for work?**
- **make errors in your work?**
- **do not work quickly enough?**

ASSIGNMENT 5

A service to all

Organisations provide products and/or services to customers and clients. They meet a need in the community and provide jobs and other benefits to employees. This assignment asks you to look at a particular organisation to see where it fits in to the local community.

YOUR TASKS

1 **Select an organisation you are familiar with and make a note of its:**

   - **name**
   - **location**
   - **main business**
   - **ownership.**

2 **Describe what it provides to meet customer needs: Goods or services? Cheap or expensive? Delivery of goods? Special offers?**

3 **Find out how many people it employs. What sort of jobs do they do? Draw up a list of the main jobs and say what they are like and how many people do them. For example:**

JOB	WHAT THEY ARE LIKE	HOW MANY
Office work	Clerical jobs and telesales	35

4 **Find out about other benefits it provides for employees and make a note of them. This will include staff discounts, flexitime and other such benefits.**

5 **Find out if it helps the local community in other ways, e.g. by giving money to charities, providing goods for prizes or sponsoring local sports teams. Even small businesses can and do help the community in various ways.**

ASSIGNMENT 6

Applying for a job

You will be applying for jobs in the near future. It may be for a work experience placement, a part-time job, or a full-time job at the end of the course. If you are in a job you may apply for a promotion at your place of work or with a different employer.

YOUR TASKS

1 Think about the sort of jobs you would like to do. Read job adverts, seek careers advice and find out about training and careers in organisations in which you may like to work.

2 Choose a job which you are interested in.

3 Obtain details from a few firms of jobs that might suit you. Look at the documents they send you and see if you think the job would suit you. What sort of an image of the employer do you get from the documents?

4 List your achievements, qualifications, skills, qualities and experience. You may find it helpful to get someone else to look at this list and see if you have missed anything.

5 Prepare a cv using a word processor, being positive about what you have to offer. One of the advantages of a word processor is that you can change things easily so make the cv a general one that you can adapt for any job you apply for. It would be good practice to take the details of the jobs that you got earlier and alter the cv to suit each of them.

6 Now, if you wish, you could practise being interviewed through role play. If someone is able to make a video of your interview you would gain much by watching yourself and noting what you do well and what improvements you could make.

D

Part D aims to:

- *Tell you the Options open to you after completing your BTEC First Diploma in Business and Finance.*
- *Tell you where you can get help and advice to decide on your future career.*

Where next?

When you have successfully completed your BTEC First Diploma in Business and Finance you need to decide what you want to do next. This part of the book aims to help you to decide on this important issue.

There is only one unit in this section of the book, Unit 21, Options after BTEC First.

OPTIONS AFTER BTEC FIRST

21

In order to help you to decide what to do next, this unit looks at three stages in deciding what to do after your BTEC First.

1 Finding out what is available to you.
2 Deciding what suits you and what you want to do.
3 Choosing your next step.

Once you have finished your course you have to decide what to do next. There are quite a few options open to you:

- Get a job (or try for a new job).
- Go on to BTEC National.
- Go on to another course.
- Work for yourself.

1 Finding out what is available to you

The options available mentioned above are probably the main ones available – self employment, a BTEC National or another college course, a job, or a combination of a course and working. This section is to help you to find out what is on offer for you.

You looked at action plans in Unit 3 of this book. Look back at that section now and consider what your aims are. Make a note of them.

ACTIVITY

An action plan is a bit like a map of a journey – it helps you see where you are at the moment and to decide where you want to go. It may also fill in some of the route for you.

Where can you get information?

Your college will have a careers service and they will be able to tell you about the various courses that you can take after a BTEC First. Obviously you could look at going on to the next course in the BTEC system – the BTEC National Diploma in Business and Finance. This is:

- a two-year course
- part-time or full-time
- A level equivalent
- a route to polytechnic, university or other study

and there are quite a lot of other courses that will then be open to you at college. If you have been sent on the BTEC First by your employer they may be prepared to help you to carry on to further study and you should discuss this with your training officer or manager to find out the courses they feel would be most helpful to you.

ACTIVITY

Make a list of the courses that you could go on to, the main features of the course, and what they would offer you. An example is included.

COURSE	FEATURES	BENEFITS
BTEC National Certificate	Part-time Can go on to HNC Options	Help with my job May help with promotion Can choose what options I like

If you are thinking about looking for a job you will need different sorts of information – where to look for work, what is involved in different jobs and what help you can get. The best place to start is probably the local job centre or your careers service – they will be able to provide you with leaflets that will tell you about different jobs, give you tips on how to apply and make a good impression as well as advice on the sort of jobs available. Different sources of information include:

- *Careers service* – advice and help on the choice of a career as well as useful information on how to apply and what different jobs involve.

- *Job centre* – useful information and advice; job vacancies displayed.
- *Banks* – often provide leaflets on starting work.
- *College careers service* – may be able to provide counselling on applying for jobs and even to arrange mock interviews so you can get feedback on how to improve.
- *Job agencies* – have lists of office vacancies and will advise you as to the sort of job you could apply for.

ACTIVITY

Make a list of the main types of job that you think would interest you and label a folder for each of them. Go round the sources of information listed above and gather all the information you can. File it under the appropriate job and then look through each file. Does it sound like the job for you?

If you are thinking of working for yourself there are a lot of places which will give you helpful information – banks, building societies, local business clubs or enterprise trusts will all provide information on what help is available and how to go about setting up business. This is something you will need to research very thoroughly and be very sure of – take advantage of as much advice as you can get and talk to people who have set up their own business to make sure this is right for you. If it is, and you are sure you can make a go of it, it can be a very rewarding way to make a living, but a risky one for a young person.

2 Deciding what suits you and what you want to do

When you have got all the information you need you have to decide what to do. There may not be much of a decision to make – you know you want to stay on at college and then go on to polytechnic or university or the firm has told you they want you to do a BTEC National. The decision might be forced on you – if you want a particular job and you need more qualifications you will have to get them, or if there are no jobs available that you want you may need to return to study. For some people, though, there is a difficult decision to make – all of the options have their advantages.

ACTIVITY

Make a list of the options you think are open to you and the advantages and disadvantages of each one. An example is included.

OPTIONS	PLUS POINTS	MINUS POINTS
Stay at college	Get more qualifications Like college	Short of money

It may be useful to get advice from other people – talk to friends who are in jobs about what they see as the good points of work and what the problems are. Talk to people on any courses you are considering – why did they do the course, is it useful, are they enjoying it? Talk to friends and family and get their views but, in the end, *you* have to make the decision. It is *your* future, *you* decide what is best for you.

3 Choosing your next step

Once you have decided what you want to do you need to sort it out.

If you want a job

- Go to the job centre, find out if local papers advertise jobs and if there are any employment agencies which deal with the sort of work you want to do.
- Visit the job centre and the employment agencies and make a point of reading the paper, either at home or in the local library.
- Make a note of any jobs suitable for you and send off for details of them.
- Find out what help is available (e.g. a job club, mock interviews or counselling on job applications) and use it.
- Apply promptly for the jobs you are interested in. Keep a copy of the application and file it for future reference.

If you want to stay at college

- Find out who is responsible for the course you want to do and either go to see them or write to them explaining why you want to do the course and asking for an application form.
- Apply early. Make sure the form is neat, that you have filled in all the details, and that you have given accurate address and telephone numbers so that you can be contacted easily.

If you want to work for yourself

- Get all the help and information you can. Read the leaflets and books. Talk to people in their own businesses.
- Work out if it is possible. It is no use planning to go into something you cannot do or cannot afford.
- Try to do a short course on starting a business. This will give you a lot of valuable information. Try your college.
- Do a full business plan and ask other people to look over it, help you with it and provide advice. Make sure it is well presented.

- Find out what help is available if you do set up on your own. Ask at the job centre about the Enterprise Allowance Scheme and ask about premises at the local council – some give special deals to small businesses.
- Ask for trade discount if there is anything you have to buy.

Summary

1 *When you successfully complete your BTEC First Diploma in Business and Finance you could obtain employment, work for yourself, start another course such as a BTEC National in Business and Finance, or get a job and study part-time.*

2 *Your College Careers Service can help you to decide what to do next.*

3 *If you are a part-time student with a job, your Training Officer will be able to help you decide.*

4 *Your local job centre and Careers Service can give you advice and information on employment opportunities, job applications and careers. Job agencies also provide information on job opportunities.*

5 *Banks, building societies, local business clubs or Enterprise Agencies can provide information and support to people who wish to set up their own business.*